ROGER THAT!

THE FOUR
THAT CAME BEFORE

XXXVI VS. RAMS (2001)

20-17

XXXVIII VS. PANTHERS (2003)

32-29

XXXIX VS. EAGLES (2004)

24-21

XLIX VS. SEAHAWKS (2014)

28-24

Julian Edelman takes the field, one more title in sight.

BOOK STAFF

EDITOR Janice Page

ASSISTANT EDITOR/WRITER Ron Driscoll

ART DIRECTOR Rena Anderson Sokolow

DESIGNER Cynthia Daniels

RESEARCHERS/PROOFREADERS Paul Colton, Tim Flynn, William Herzog, James Matte

PHOTOGRAPHERS

THE BOSTON GLOBE Barry Chin: front cover, 4, 15, 19, 28, 29, 34, 38, 41, 43, 54, 58, 59, 67, 71, 79, 81, 105, 114, 121; Jim Davis: 7, 14, 22, 36, 40, 46, 52, 56, 74, 75, 77, 83, 89, 91, 97, 102, 103, 104; Stan Grossfeld: 2, 26, 43, 45, 50, 106, 108; Matthew Lee: 60, 69, 73, 85, 93; John Tlumacki: 62, 95, 101; John Blanding: 42; Bill Greene: 42; Frank O'Brien: 100; Jonathan Wiggs: 117.

ADDITIONAL PHOTOS COURTESY OF
AP/Wide World Photos, 1; 12, 15, 19 (Darron Cummings); 20 (Matt Slocum); 64 (Jason DeCrow); 65 (Richard Drew); 87 (Bill Kostroun); 119 (Winslow Townson); 124 (Tim Donnelly); 127 (Jae C. Hong). Getty Images, back cover; 15, 128 (Ezra Shaw); 16, 24, 110 (Kevin C. Cox); 30, 127 (Timothy A. Clary); 50 (file); 107 (Tom Pennington).

With special thanks to Boston Globe publisher John W. Henry, chief executive officer Doug Franklin, managing director Linda Pizzuti Henry, and editor Brian McGrory; Joe Sullivan and the Boston Globe sports department; Bill Greene and the Globe photo department; Lisa Tuite and the Globe library staff; Jane Bowman, Erin Maghran, and Globe marketing; Mitch Rogatz, Kristine Anstrats, and the entire team at Triumph Books; Chris Jackson and Quad/Graphics of Taunton; Todd Shuster, Lane Zachary, and Zachary Shuster Harmsworth Literary Agency.

At right Tom Brady strikes a familiar pose as he and his sons, Jack and Ben, celebrate Brady's fifth Super Bowl victory, the result of an unprecedented comeback from a 25-point deficit.

Back cover Tom Brady, who won his fourth Super Bowl MVP, shakes hands with NFL commissioner Roger Goodell, who meted out the four-game Deflategate suspension to the Patriots quarterback and received raucous boos during the trophy ceremony.

The Boston Globe

Copyright © 2017 by The Boston Globe

No part of this publication may be reproduced, stored in a retrieval system, or transmitted in any form by any means, electronic, mechanical, photocopying, or otherwise, without prior written permission of the publisher, Triumph Books LLC, 814 North Franklin Street; Chicago, Illinois 60610.

This book is available in quantity at special discounts for your group or organization.

For further information, contact:

Triumph Books LLC
814 North Franklin Street
Chicago, Illinois 60610
Phone: (312) 337-0747
www.triumphbooks.com
@TriumphBooks
Printed in U.S.A.
ISBN: 978-1-62937-298-3

This is an unofficial publication. This book is in no way affiliated with, licensed by, or endorsed by the NFL or the New England Patriots·

TRIUMPH
BOOKS

TRIUMPHBOOKS.COM

CONTENTS

INTRODUCTION

BY JOHN POWERS / Globe Staff

This one wasn't simply about revenge, although being handed the championship trophy by NFL commissioner Roger Goodell, their chief prosecutor and persecutor, was supremely sweet. And it wasn't about redemption after the previous campaign ended abruptly in Denver, although this season's mile-high payback undoubtedly was fulfilling. » The Patriots' fifth Super Bowl triumph, achieved in Houston with a 34-28 overtime shocker over the Atlanta Falcons in the greatest comeback in postseason history, primarily was about persistence and posterity, a special place in professional history for owner Robert Kraft's franchise, for coach Bill Belichick and for quarterback Tom Brady, who collected an especially prized ring — one for the thumb. "We're bringing this sucker home!" declared Brady, brandishing the Lombardi Trophy after leading his teammates back from the dead with 31 unanswered points. » New England, appearing in its seventh title match in 16 seasons, won this one despite missing Brady for the first four games, despite losing favorite target Rob Gronkowski to back surgery in November and despite trading away two Pro Bowl defenders and losing another to retirement. » The team still managed to win a record eighth straight AFC East crown with its best record (14-2) in half a dozen years as a rejiggered offense with newcomers Martellus Bennett, Chris Hogan, Malcolm Mitchell and Michael Floyd averaged four touchdowns a game and the restocked defense led the league in fewest points allowed for the first time in 13 years. "Preparation, practice, execution," said Belichick, who set a record for most Super Bowl victories by a head coach. "There's no magic wand." » The Patriots prevailed because they stubbornly stuck to the game plan that has made them the most successful franchise of the millennium: Do Your Job. "It's not like they're so much better than everyone else," said a Texans executive, whose club was hammered 27-0 by a third-string quarterback. "They just execute. They always execute."

Even without the man who'd been calling signals for them since 2001. "I'm not going to lie, it's like one of your buddies going to jail," said receiver Julian Edelman after Brady was suspended for his role in the Deflategate saga.

Yet with backups Jimmy Garoppolo and Jacoby Brissett filling in, New England still won its first three outings before being blanked at home for the first time since 1993. "We're 3-1," remarked Bennett. "Nobody's panicking. We're still the Patriots."

Still, after star linebacker Jamie Collins was traded to Cleveland on Halloween, observers were wondering what Belichick was up to. "Shheeshhh," tweeted former defensive end Chandler Jones, who'd been dealt to Arizona during the offseason. But the defense, bolstered by its exceptional secondary, performed more than creditably. And when Brady returned refreshed and resolute, his star-spangled comrades won 11 of their final 12 regular-season contests, subduing the nemesis Ravens and losing only to the Seahawks after being stopped at the goal line with 11 seconds to play.

The finale at Miami was telling. The Patriots had squandered home-field advantage by losing there in 2015. This time they clinched it throughout with a 35-14 runaway to complete a perfect road slate.

"We got to right a lot of wrongs that we messed up last year," said Logan Ryan. But despite a first-round bye and what appeared to be an easy rematch with Houston, they were prepared for the hard road to the Super Bowl. "You've got to earn the right to come back to work," said safety Devin McCourty.

Scoring 70 points against the Texans and Steelers earned them a ticket to the title match, where New England defied mathematical reason and savored yet another confetti bath and its most satisfying chunk of jewelry after James White bulled his way into the end zone. "This is unequivocally the sweetest," Kraft crowed. Roger that. ■

Patriots receiver Danny Amendola (80) jaws with Atlanta cornerback Brian Poole in the second quarter.

LI

SUPER BOWL

34.

BY DAN SHAUGHNESSY / Globe Staff

It will take weeks, months, maybe years to fully absorb this one, but given all the layers of drama, emotion, and improbability, the Patriots' 34-28 overtime Super Bowl victory over the Atlanta Falcons in Super Bowl LI might very well be the greatest moment in Boston sports history. And that, folks, is saying something. » Super Bowl LI at massive NRG Stadium was supposed to be all about revenge and a Roger Goodell trophy moment, but it wound up being the greatest comeback in Super Bowl history and a victory against which all others — in every sport — will forever be measured. » "Thanks to all our fans," said Tom Brady, while he held the Lombardi Trophy. "You've been with us all year and we're going to bring this sucker home!" » The Patriots fell behind the Falcons, 21-0, in the first half. They trailed, 28-3, with less than three minutes to play in the third quarter. Forget about revenge for Deflategate penalties, it looked as if the Patriots were going to be embarrassed. And then, they scored 31 unanswered points in less than two full quarters. » We can »18

6 Points, the margin of victory for the Patriots, the largest in any of their five Super Bowl wins.

93 The number of teams in NFL playoff history who held a 19-point lead in the final quarter before Super Bowl LI. All of them won.

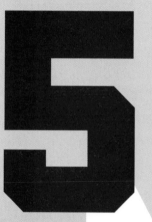

5 Tom Brady joins Bart Starr (3 NFL titles, 2 Super Bowls) as the only two QBs with five championships.

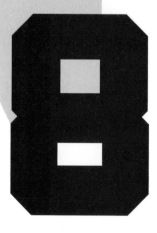

8 Matt Ryan became the eighth consecutive NFL MVP who has played in the Super Bowl to lose, joining, among others, Cam Newton (2015), Tom Brady (2007), and Kurt Warner (2001).

James White caught a Super Bowl-record 14 passes and became the first player since Terrell Davis in 1998 to score three touchdowns in the Super Bowl.

Tom Brady has a record seven fourth-quarter comebacks in the playoffs.

The Patriots have 0 first-quarter points in seven Super Bowls with Bill Belichick and Tom Brady.

Bill Belichick's five NFL titles are one behind Curly Lambeau and George Halas, who won six titles each.

34-28

NE	0	3	6	19	6
ATL	0	21	7	0	0

Tom Brady leads teammates onto the field for the seventh time in a Super Bowl, the most appearances in the game for any player.

Tom Brady is down — and the Patriots appear to be out — after a pick-six by Atlanta's Robert Alford (23), combined with a TD throw from Matt Ryan (2) to Austin Hooper (81), as well as scores from Tevin Coleman (26) and Devonta Freeman.

James White helps the Patriots start their comeback by beating Atlanta's Jalen Collins for a 5-yard TD catch, capping a 13-play, third-quarter drive.

FROM 9 • officially retire all arguments about Greatest Of All Time. Brady is the greatest quarterback. And Bill Belichick is the greatest coach. They are the first pair to win five Super Bowls. And no one will ever forget how they got this latest one.

Playing in silent fury following his September suspension, but inspired by the presence of his ill mother, who hadn't seen him play all season, Brady threw for 466 yards and led a 91-yard, game-tying touchdown drive at the end of regulation. He was named Super Bowl MVP for a record

'IT'S ALL ABOUT THESE PLAYERS. THEY'RE TOUGH AND THEY COMPETE'

fourth time.

Belichick, meanwhile, repeatedly outsmarted the Atlanta coaching staff. He Did His Job. The Hoodie made the other guys panic. And he made some history along the way.

The victory was clinched at 10:25 p.m. EST when third-year running back James White slashed through, and bounced off, a pack of helpless Falcons defenders to finish off a 75-yard, four-minute touchdown drive in overtime. The poor, pitiful Falcons never touched the ball in the extra session. It's always a mistake to lose the coin toss to the Patriots.

Goodell could hardly be heard over the boos while he presented the trophy to Patriots owner Robert Kraft. The Commish handed over the ¬Lombardi, shook hands with Kraft, then bolted. He shook hands with Brady on the confetti-littered stadium lawn.

"Two years ago when we won in Arizona, I told our fans that was the sweetest one of all," said Kraft. "But a lot has transpired.

I want to say to our fans and our brilliant coaching staff, this is unequivocally the sweetest, and I'm proud to say for the fifth time we are all Patriots, and tonight for the fifth time, the Patriots are world champions."

"It's all about these players," added Belichick. "They're tough and they compete."

The Falcons were supposed to be mere speed bumps on the Patriots' road to immortality, but they turned out to be just plain speedy. Atlanta forced a couple of Patriot turnovers in the second quarter and capitalized with three touchdowns to take what should have been an insurmountable lead.

"It was hard to imagine us winning it at that point," admitted Brady. "When we got the ball in the second half, it was tough to slow us down."

The first quarter was somewhat shocking. Nobody scored, with each team punting twice. Then came two Patriots turnovers and three second-quarter Falcons touchdowns.

The third of Atlanta's three quick scores came when Brady was picked off by Robert Alford, who dashed a breathtaking 82 yards into the other end zone. Brady was the last man who had a chance to tackle the Falcons cornerback, and it was not a pretty sight. It was the first pick-six of Brady's illustrious postseason career.

The Patriots managed only a 41-yard field goal in the final seconds of the first half, and it got worse for New England in the third quarter. The Patriots had to punt on their first series, and Ryan took over, hitting Tevin Coleman for a 6-yard touchdown pass to make it 28-3 with 8:31 left in the third.

"I wasn't thinking much," said Brady. "I was just thinking we had to score."

Belichick emptied his bag of tricks the rest of the way. On their first touchdown TD drive late in

the third quarter, the Patriots went for it on fourth and 3 from near midfield and converted. Brady later saved the series with a 15-yard scramble. A 5-yard TD pass to White cut the margin to 28-9 with 2:06 left in the third. When Stephen Gostkowski missed the extra point, it really felt like this might not be New England's night.

After a Patriots field goal cut the margin to 28-12, Dont'a Hightower forced a Ryan fumble and the Patriots took over on the Atlanta 25-yard line. It was still a two-score game. Seconds later, Brady hit Danny Amendola (6 yards) in the end zone to make it 28-18. Two-point conversions were critical, and the Patriots got the first one they needed on a direct snap to White to make it 28-20 with 5:56 left.

You could feel the Falcons panicking. They advanced the ball to the New England 22 and could have sealed the game with a chip-shot field goal but moved backward on a sack and a penalty and wound up punting.

This was New England's last stand. And Brady made it count. He moved his team 91 yards in 10 plays. White's 1-yard TD run cut it to 28-26, and then came a 2-point conversion pass to Danny Amendola.

In overtime, the Patriots called heads — as they always do — and the coin came up heads. Sudden death. The Falcons never had a chance. They still don't know what hit them, but New England fans recognized it. It was the 10th championship for a Boston sports team since the Patriots broke a 15-year city drought with their first title in 2002, and possibly the sweetest. ■

Dont'a Hightower roars in on Falcons quarterback Matt Ryan for a critical forced fumble in the fourth quarter that was recovered by New England's Alan Branch, leading to the Patriots' second touchdown.

Julian Edelman is upended by Atlanta's Philip Wheeler after making the first of his five catches in the game, which accounted for 87 total yards.

FLIP THE SCRIPT

Tom Brady compiled The Drive. Julian Edelman made The Catch.

And the Patriots have The Hill to thank for their victory over the Falcons.

The hill sits on the back of the Patriots' practice field at Gillette Stadium, and Bill Belichick makes the players run it every day at the end of practice.

"We all bitch and complain about it," receiver Julian Edelman said. "But hey, we did it, we put in the work, we put in the conditioning."

The Patriots ran the Falcons ragged all game, and it paid off in a wild fourth quarter and overtime. Trailing, 28-20, with 3:30 on the clock, Super Bowl MVP Tom Brady led the Patriots 91 yards for the game-tying touchdown, then marched the offense 75 yards down the field in overtime to pull for the win.

"I think for sure we ran out of gas some," Falcons coach Dan Quinn said.

The Patriots didn't, even after running 93 plays, gaining 546 yards, and holding the ball for 40:31. They rose to the occasion, pulling off the most improbable and largest comeback victory in Super Bowl history.

"We all brought each other back. We never felt out of it," Brady said.

Brady threw for a Super Bowl-record 466 yards in being named the game's MVP, and once again, he was at his best in the game's most crucial moments, leading the Patriots to three touchdowns and a field goal on their last four possessions.

James White set a Super Bowl record with 14 receptions, and caught 4 of 5 passes on the tying and winning drives for 23 yards, capping both drives with rushing scores.

"We just kept going to him,"

Brady said, "so I think that speaks for itself."

The tying drive didn't begin well. Brady twice threw incomplete before hitting Chris Hogan for 16 yards, and two plays later found Malcolm Mitchell for 11 yards.

Then came The Catch.

"I don't know how he caught it," said Brady. "I don't think he does, either."

The Patriots have seen it three times before — all against them. David Tyree's miracle catch in Super Bowl 42. Mario Manningham's toe-tapping wonder in Super Bowl 47. Jermaine Kearse's circus catch in Super Bowl 49.

This time, it was Edelman's turn. Coming from the right slot, Edelman beat Falcons cornerback Robert Alford on a deep post over the middle. But Alford was able to bat the ball in the air, and Edelman converged on it with three Falcon defenders. Edelman fought to get his hands under the ball, then bobbled it. Then he got his hands under it again, millimeters before it hit the ground.

The officials signaled a 23-yard catch to the Falcons' 41.

"It was kind of a 'flip the script' there, know what I mean?" offensive coordinator Josh McDaniels said.

Quinn immediately challenged the play. "Clearly it was a catch," Quinn said later. "But at the time I thought it was worth the challenge."

The initial ruling was confirmed, and from that point, there was no stopping Brady.

"To come back from 25 points, it's hard to imagine us winning," Brady said. "A lot of mental toughness by our team. And we're all going to remember this for the rest of our lives."

BEN VOLIN • *Globe Staff*

Patriots wide receiver Danny Amendola gathers in a fourth-quarter touchdown catch from Tom Brady to bring New England within 10 points of Atlanta, 28-18. Amendola caught eight passes for 78 yards in the game.

Julian Edelman outduels Atlanta safeties Ricardo Allen and Keanu Neal for an improbable 23-yard gain on the Patriots' game-tying scoring drive in the fourth quarter.

New England's Malcolm Mitchell and Chris Hogan celebrate and Atlanta players are deflated as the official signals James White's game-winning touchdown in overtime.

James White spikes the ball after his game-winning touchdown and is promptly tackled by teammate LeGarrette Blount (29). White scored three touchdowns and added a two-point conversion, the most points by any player in Super Bowl history.

Patriots coach Bill Belichick stands alone as the only coach to win five Super Bowls, breaking a tie with Pittsburgh's Chuck Noll. Belichick's five NFL titles leave him one behind Curly Lambeau and George Halas.

'WE DIDN'T DO A GOOD ENOUGH JOB OR A QUICK ENOUGH JOB ADAPTING TO THE CIRCUMSTANCES.'

MIKE TOMLIN · STEELERS COACH

'TOM DID WHAT TOM DOES. HE WAS LASER-FOCUSED.'

MARTELLUS BENNETT · PATRIOTS TIGHT END

AFC POSTSEASON

BY CHRISTOPHER L. GASPER / Globe Staff

From NFL house arrest to unwanted NFL house guest in Houston at Super Bowl LI, it's another "only Tom Brady" storybook tale. » Deflategate will go down as just another obstacle the quarterback had to overcome in the remarkable career he has carved out as the consummate winner. A four-game suspension designed by NFL commissioner Roger Goodell to hamper Brady's pursuit of another championship merely inspired it. » "Nah, this is my motivation right here, all these fellas in front of me," Brady said on the AFC Championship presentation stage at Gillette Stadium, disguising his real emotions far better than the Pittsburgh Steelers disguised their coverages. » We finally saw what happens when the Patriots face a legitimate AFC contender with a franchise quarterback. It's the same thing that happened to the list of unworthy and quarterback-questionable teams they mostly played over the second half of the season — they lose in resounding fashion. The AFC Championship game against the Steelers was less a competition and more a ritualistic sacrifice that sent Brady and Coach Bill Belichick to their seventh Super Bowl together. » There can be no more questioning the Patriots' eminence. The level of competition doesn't matter because Brady is on another level and the New England defense proved its stinginess was on the level in a 36-17 victory.

»39

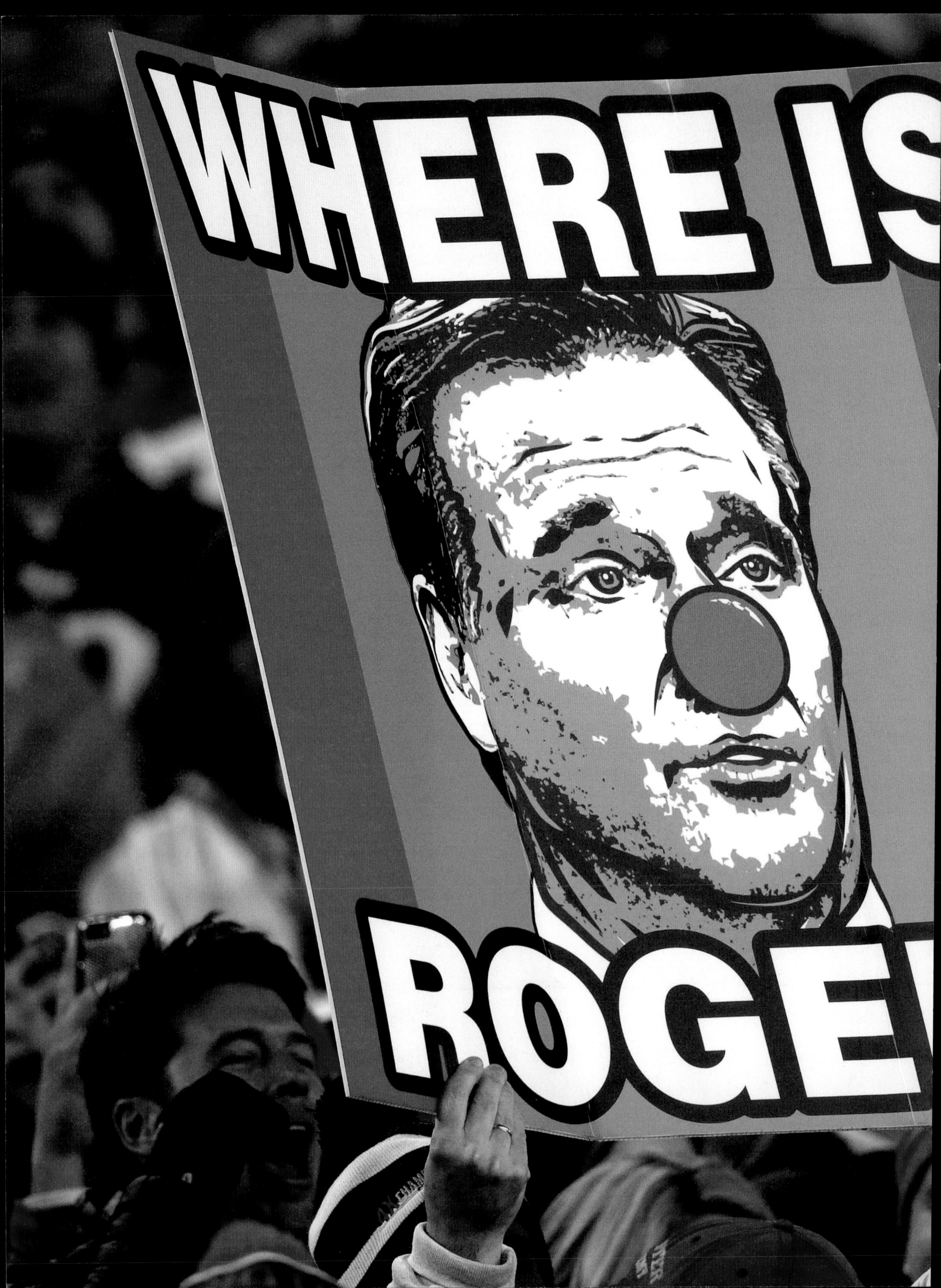
WHERE IS
ROGE

As the Patriots closed in on their ninth trip to the Super Bowl, the obvious question was the whereabouts of the NFL commissioner. The answer? Atlanta, for the NFC title game.

9

The Patriots advanced to their ninth Super Bowl, breaking a four-way tie at 8 with the Cowboys, Steelers, and Broncos.

20-4

The Patriots' home playoff record after beating Pittsburgh (16-3 at Gillette Stadium).

11

Conference Championship games played by Tom Brady, the most all-time. Gene Upshaw and George Blanda played in 10.

180

Receiving yards for Chris Hogan, most in team playoff history, eclipsing Deion Branch (153 yards vs. Denver, 2006).

36-17

PIT	0	9	0	8
NE	10	7	16	3

It worked! Tom Brady and Chris Hogan celebrate after Hogan hauled in Brady's 34-yard touchdown pass on a flea-flicker play in the second quarter.

Shea McClellin, Devin McCourty, Dont'a Hightower (54), and (somewhere in the pile) Patrick Chung, wrap up Pittsburgh's DeAngelo Williams on a goal-line stand in the second quarter. The Steelers started at the 1/2-yard line and were forced to settle for a field goal.

FROM 33 • The last time the AFC title game was held in Foxborough, back in 2015 against the Indianapolis Colts, the odious air pressure imbroglio known as Deflategate was spawned after a Brady pass was intercepted by D'Qwell Jackson. The Colts stuck a gauge in the ball, opening a Pandora's Box for the NFL.

The only thing that was deflated on this night was Pittsburgh's defense, which would have been better off had it used the Lord's Prayer as its game plan. This rematch was a complete mismatch.

The idea that the Steelers can stop Brady falls in the category of alternative facts. Bouncing back from the lowest postseason completion percentage of his career against Houston, Brady torched the Sons of the Steel Curtain, going 32 of 42 for 384 yards and three touchdowns. In seven games against the Mike Tomlin-coached Steelers, Brady has passed for 2,273 yards and 22 touchdowns with zero interceptions.

Playing in his record 11th AFC title game, Brady played the Steelers like a Stradivarius. He knew exactly what coverage they were in and exactly how to defeat it; it showed as he tied his idol Joe Montana for the most postseason games with three or more touchdowns passes (nine). He also extended his NFL record for 300-yard playoff performances to 11.

Unless you're Seattle or Denver, if you just do what you do against Brady you are doomed, especially if it's predictable zone coverages and blitzes.

"You know they did what they did," said wide receiver Julian Edelman, who had eight catches for 118 yards and a score. "And we were just able to execute today. They're a tough team. We made plays, and we have respect for their franchise. We won't get into that whole thing. They fought hard."

Pittsburgh defensive end Stephon Tuitt was a bit less diplomatic. "Yeah, he ripped us apart," said Tuitt. "We're going to watch the film and see what happened. We didn't get there and he picked us apart."

Brady was 6 of 6 for 66 yards on the Patriots' first TD drive. His last pass was a 16-yarder to a wide-open Chris Hogan in the back of the end zone on a play where the Steelers brought their inside linebackers while dropping their best pass rusher, Bud Dupree, into coverage. The result was Brady had time to post to his new Instagram account from the pocket before finding Hogan to put the Patriots up, 10-0, in the first quarter.

At that point, Brady was 10 of »40

FROM 39 • 12 for 128 yards and a touchdown. The two incompletions were a Malcolm Mitchell drop and an attempted wide receiver screen play where the snap appeared to be out of synch.

Brady just played games with the Pittsburgh defense. On the first touchdown drive, the Patriots lined up in a heavier set with fullback James Develin and running back LeGarrette Blount in the backfield and one tight end. The Steelers brought a safety down. Then Brady motioned everyone out into an empty set and hit a wide-open Hogan for a 26-yard gain.

New England's second touchdown came via a flea-flicker. Brady took the ball back from Dion Lewis and lofted a 34-yard pass to Hogan for a 17-6 lead. Brady had his choice of intended TD targets on the play.

Sensing a theme here? The Patriots receivers were often unaccompanied. Hogan finished with nine catches for 180 yards and two scores.

There might have been some Patriots fans who were a bit anxious with New England up, 17-9, at the half, but it felt like it was all under control in Foxborough with TB12 reading the Steelers' minds.

Two plays after Brady called out the Steelers' blitz, calmly slid to his right, and hit Hogan for a 39-yard gain, Blount plunged in from the 1 to make it 27-9 with 2:44 left in third quarter. Checking airfare to Houston was allowable.

"He's the best quarterback to ever play the game," said Blount.

The Steelers fumbled on the ensuing drive and Brady drove the stake through the Steelers' hearts, connecting with Edelman for a 10-yard TD on third and goal to make it 33-9. AFC Championship game over, Big Game on. ■

Eric Rowe breaks up a second-quarter pass intended for Pittsburgh's Cobi Hamilton (83), and Rob Ninkovich recovers a third-quarter Steeler fumble, setting up a Patriots touchdown by Julian Edelman.

IS THERE SUCH A THING AS

These winter weeks can be the darkest of the year. The holidays are behind us, but for the bills. The sky is often the color of a dirty sheet. Sports fans know pitchers and catchers won't report until Valentine's Day or so, and the Celtics and Bruins are grinding through the middle of their schedules, the playoffs as distant as beach-worthy weather.

Yet for the seventh time in the Bill Belichick-Tom Brady era, New England's NFL team found itself playing into February this year, capturing its fifth Super Bowl win in the new millennium.

To appease the forces of karma it seems wise to occasionally note how fortunate we are. How much we appreciate this charmed era of Boston sports fandom, with 10 championship trophies to our name since 2000. How we would never take it for granted.

But do we?

When candidate Donald Trump said, "We're going to win so much, you're going to be so sick and tired of winning" … could he have been talking about us?

"I think the early victories had a larger emotional pop because they were unique and novel," said Adam H. Naylor, a Boston University professor of sports psychology, speaking of the Patriots' first Super Bowl win after the 2001 season and the curse-busting 2004 World Series.

Now, "it's not the same … because it's what is supposed to happen," he said, referring to all the winning that goes on around here. "All of our kids know what it's like to win. I think the historians of the sports don't take it for granted, but we've been on such a run," Naylor said.

It's reasonable there would be "a little" taking-for-granted going on. "My gut wishes not," he said.

It's hard to imagine any lack of appreciation among longtime Patriots fans who withstood the extended loseapalooza before Robert Kraft bought the team in 1994, those who remember wishing Rod Rust would bench Marc Wilson for Tommy Hodson at old Schaefer/Sullivan/Foxboro stadium, the venue with the architectural charm of a Soviet prison camp, but fewer amenities. Back then, when they referred to the cheap seats as "the nosebleeds" it was because you might get punched. The fandom was in a foul mood.

Everything has changed.

Since 2000, the Patriots have earned seven Super Bowl berths and won five; the Red Sox have won the three World Series in which they appeared, in 2004, 2007, 2013; the Celtics have played in two NBA Finals, winning in 2008; and the Bruins made two Stanley Cup Finals, winning in 2011.

It has meant job security for duck boat drivers, but so much more.

For fans, "there becomes an identification with a team's progression that really taps into this sense of progress and mobility for all of us," said Dr. Ericka Bohnel, a psychologist and Patriots fan. "In times when people are feeling taxed and fearful of what is next, there is emboldenment that happens by aligning ourselves with a sports team."

It may be we are so used to winning around here, we forget how losing can warp the psyche of an entire community.

Not long ago we were all pessimists, down on our sports selves, believers of curses. A little like Cincinnati, which has not sniffed a championship since the Reds won the World Series in 1990.

Here's an experiment. Make one phone call to one random Cincy sports bar. How about O'Malley's in the Alley? Ask to speak to the nearest local sport fan and they'll probably hand the phone to somebody like Fritz Whaley, a 28-year-old bartender.

Tell him you're looking for the sports opposite of Boston.

"That's definitely us," Whaley confirmed instantly. No pride-infused pushback whatsoever. "Five straight years of playoffs and not one win. Pretty embarrassing."

While Boston fans are clinking glasses of Super Bowl punch, the locals at O'Malley's will be downing domestic beer with a shot of Jameson. It's called the "Harambe," after the gorilla gunned down at the Cincinnati Zoo. It's what they have to work with at the moment.

Like a lot of fans around the country, Whaley finds the Patriots infuriating.

"It's just — I'm tired of seeing them win," he said. "Why can't we have Belichick? Can't we have somebody who finds random players, sticks them together, and takes them to the playoffs and Super Bowls?"

For New England fans who know nothing but winning, Whaley says this: "You guys are lucky. Come to Cincinnati and feel my pain for a little while, where we have so much high hopes for the season, and then when you see what happens, it's so deflating."

Pause.

"No pun intended. Ha ha ha."

MARK ARSENAULT • *Globe Staff (with Cristela Guerra and Travis Andersen contributing)*

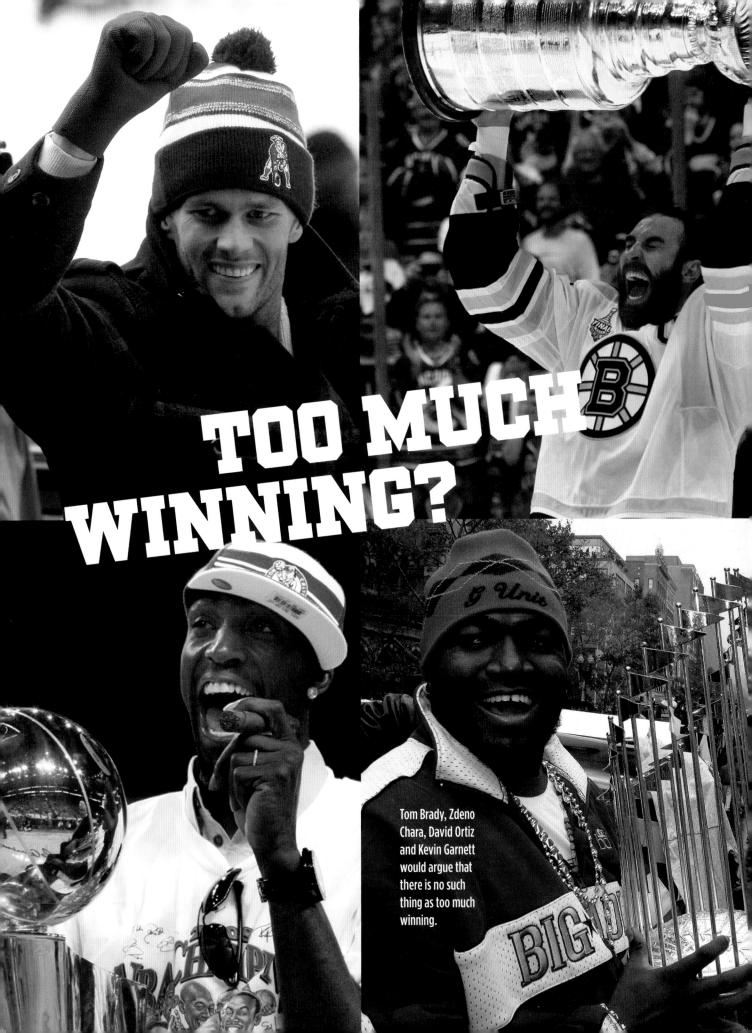

TOO MUCH WINNING?

Tom Brady, Zdeno Chara, David Ortiz and Kevin Garnett would argue that there is no such thing as too much winning.

The Patriots celebrate their return to the Super Bowl, as Tom Brady (32 of 42, 384 yards, three touchdowns) joins his teammates after the dismantling of the Steelers.

Running back LeGarrette Blount shares the Lamar Hunt Trophy, signifying the Patriots' ninth AFC championship, with Gillette Stadium fans.

DIVI

'WE MADE PLAYS
WHEN WE HAD TO,
BUT IF WE WANT TO
KEEP WINNING AND
MOVE ON, WE CAN'T
PLAY LIKE THAT.'

JULIAN EDELMAN

SION

BY CHRISTOPHER L. GASPER / Globe Staff

The end result was the desired one for Tom Brady and the Patriots, but the performance left something to be desired. The latter is what lingered in the singularly focused mind of Brady. » The Patriots scored enough points to make the folks in Las Vegas look prescient with their 16-point spread, but the AFC divisional-round playoff win over the Houston Texans at Gillette Stadium didn't come with any style points for Brady and the offense. The scoreboard told a story of a *fait accompli* outcome, a 34-16 Patriots victory. The reality of the game told another tale for TB12 and the Patriots, one that didn't meet their lofty expectations. That was evident by Brady's downcast demeanor in his postgame press conference. » This was good enough to win, but it wasn't good enough for Brady and the sterling-silver standard known as the Lombardi Trophy he lives by. He knows that. What a luxury it is for Brady and the Patriots to be able to self-flagellate and self-deprecate after a win that put them in the AFC Championship game for a record sixth straight season. It was also a luxury to be facing the offensively-challenged Texans. The Patriots knew they wouldn't be so fortunate in the AFC title game. » The statistic that has always defined Brady is wins. He got his 23rd playoff victory in 32 tries. That was the good. The bad was that Brady registered the lowest completion percentage »53

Dion Lewis looks back, but no one is gaining on him as he becomes the first Patriot to return a kickoff for a touchdown in the team's postseason history. It was one of three TDs for Lewis in the game.

34-16

HOU	3	10	0	3
NE	14	3	7	10

FROM 49 • of his playoff career (47.4) and matched his regular-season interception total of two in 12 games in just three quarters against the Texans' top-ranked defense. Brady was 18 of 38 for 287 yards with two touchdowns and two interceptions.

"That [stinks]," said Brady.

Granted, one of the interceptions was the fault of Bill Belichick pet project Michael Floyd, who let a second-quarter pass go through his hands and into the arms of A.J. Bouye. But this wasn't Brady at his best. He was hit, harassed, and forced to hold the ball more than he would like.

In the second half, he was 10 of 23 for 142 yards with a TD and another deflected pass-turned-interception that was his fault.

Brady was in no mood to celebrate making it to his record 11th AFC title game, breaking a tie with Raiders legends George Blanda and Gene Upshaw for the most conference title game appearances.

"I think we've just got to learn from it. I think this team did a good job playing against us. That's a good team," said Brady. "They had some good rushers, and they have some good guys in coverage. They had a pretty good plan. … You add our poor execution on top of that and add our turnovers on top of that.

"You know it just doesn't feel great because we work pretty hard to play a lot better than we played."

It turned out the Texans were not quite the willing Foxborough Foil for Brady and Co. that was expected.

Belichick disciples Bill O'Brien, Houston's head coach, and Romeo Crennel, the Texans' defensive coordinator, acquitted themselves quite well, much better than in the 27-0 beatdown the Patriots gave them with third-string rookie quarterback Jacoby Brissett at the controls back in September. The Texans kept their streak of not allowing a 300-yard passer all season intact.

If only they had competent and capable quarterback play to complement their defensive effort, this might have been a playoff thriller. Instead, they had Brock Osweiler (23 of 40 for 197 yards with a touchdown and three »55

New England linebacker Dont'a Hightower takes down Houston receiver DeAndre Hopkins in the first quarter. Hightower led the Patriots with five tackles and three assists.

Tom Brady scoots out of the pocket in the second quarter. Brady ran four times for minus-1 yard and was hounded into two sacks and two interceptions by the Houston defense.

FROM 51 • interceptions), which is like bringing a rock to a gunfight.

As it was, it was an uncomfortable evening for the Patriots for too long.

It was 24-16 with 14:51 left in the fourth quarter after Nick Novak drilled a 46-yard field goal. The Houston score was set up by Brady's second interception.

He tried to whip a pass in to Julian Edelman, who had a big night with eight catches for 137 yards, but it was deflected and intercepted by Houston safety Andre Hal at the Patriots 40 with 41 seconds left in the third quarter.

It marked the ninth time in Brady's postseason career that he tossed two or more interceptions in a game. The Patriots were 4-4 in the previous eight instances.

But after the Patriots were forced to punt when Brady threw behind an open Edelman on third and 7, Robert Pattinson-look-alike Osweiler ushered in the twilight of the Texans' season by throwing an interception to Logan Ryan at the Houston 29. Two plays later, Dion Lewis bounced in from the 1 for his third touchdown of the game with 12:16 to go, and the Patriots were safe from the ignominy of one of the worst playoff losses of the Belichick-Brady era.

It wasn't all bad for Brady. He connected on six pass plays of 20 yards or more, his most in a playoff game. TB12 appeared to seize control of the game on the Patriots' second drive of the third quarter, marching 90 yards in nine plays to take a 24-13 lead. Brady hit 6 of 7 passes on the drive, the last of which was a 19-yard score to running back James White.

But the offense went punt, interception, punt after that until Logan Ryan rolled out the red carpet to the end zone with his interception.

"It was just one of those nights where we just never got into a rhythm on offense," said Brady.

I asked Brady at his locker if there was a line between being focused and being fixated, if he and the Patriots were too tight.

"I don't think we were tight," said Brady. "We just didn't execute very well."

They executed well enough to win, but not well enough to feel good about it. ∎

Devin McCourty steps in front of Houston's DeAndre Hopkins to snag an underthrown Brock Osweiler pass, and Dion Lewis (33) celebrates his third score of the night with a leaping spike.

Duron Harmon returns a Houston interception for 31 yards in the fourth quarter to help send the Patriots to their NFL-record sixth straight conference championship game.

SEA

'THIS YEAR IT'S JUST BEEN A LOT OF MENTAL TOUGHNESS. TO BE 8-0 ON THE ROAD IS SO TOUGH IN THE NFL.'

TOM BRADY

SON

BY RON DRISCOLL

When the season began, a critical question dogged the Patriots in their pursuit of a fifth world title. How would they survive without Tom Brady, who in mid-July had finally abandoned his legal battle over "Deflategate" and accepted a four-game suspension? » When Brady returned, his team had gone 3-1, but that Week 4 loss to Buffalo (their first home shutout in 23 years) ramped up the emotion of his return and ensured that the nasty, nearly two-year feud — at once public and personal — would continue between the team and the NFL, embodied by Roger Goodell. » The Patriots nearly ran the table on Brady's return, going 11-1 — with the only loss coming in Week 10 to Seattle. And although the game ended with New England perched on the Seattle 1-yard line, the consensus was that the Patriot defense had come up short, by allowing 31 points to their Super Bowl XLIX adversaries. This was also their first game after the surprising trade of former All-Pro linebacker Jamie Collins. » No Collins, no problem, and they somehow also absorbed the loss of all-world tight end Rob Gronkowski, who suffered a back injury against Seattle. They tightened up defensively, climbing to No. 1 in the league in scoring defense, and ended the season on a seven-game win streak. "Around here you're either getting better or you're getting worse," said linebacker Dont'a Hightower. It's the Patriot Way. ◼

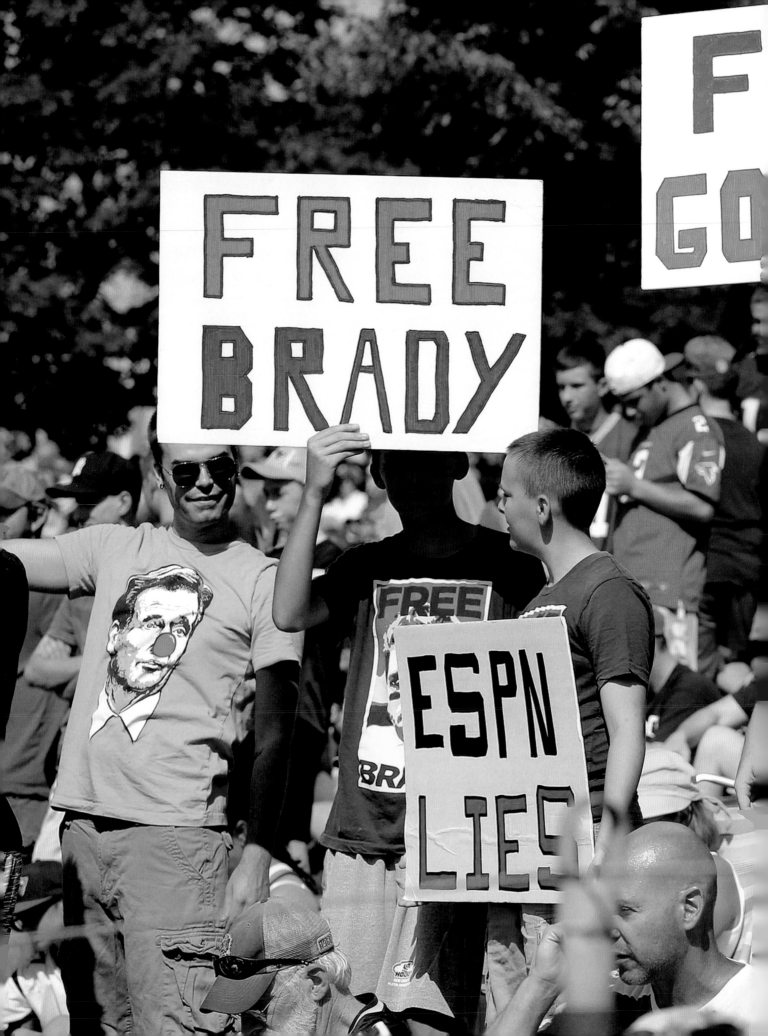

Opinions flowed more freely than optimism as the New England Patriots opened training camp in Foxborough on July 28.

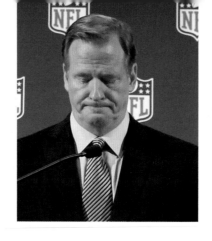

There were no fighting words from the quarterback as he (sort of) addressed his four-game suspension in the 2014 scandal known as Deflategate.

Tom Brady speaks! Stop the presses. Freeze Twitter. Close the New York Stock Exchange for 10 minutes. Interrupt all Trump coverage.

Brady ended his six-month silence at a Patriots practice on the morning of Aug. 5, 2016, when he took eight questions from the local football media for approximately five minutes. It was a shoutdown frenzy, and Tom found it easier to answer "How much did you rely on your family to get through the whole ordeal?" than "Why did you drop the appeal when you did?"

When Brady was asked what went into his mid-July decision to drop the appeal of his four-game suspension, he started with "It was just a personal decision," then shifted into Patriotspeak Overdrive: "I try to come out here and focus on what I need to do to get better and help our team. I'll be excited to be back when I'm back. I'll be cheering our team on and hopefully we go out and win every game."

Roger that, Tom.

It's safe to say that Dan Hausle, Mike Wallace, and Edward R. Murrow were not acknowledged in the scrum. Brady wasn't going to take questions from anyone asking "Did you do it?" or "What was up with the cellphone?" In soccer parlance, this was "a friendly." As breaking news, it wasn't much. Still, it ran live on ESPN and was replayed less than an hour later.

Brady has learned a thing or two about the Patriot Way in his 17 seasons in Foxborough. He knows it's always Do Your Job, and Team Above Self and Next Man Up and every other cliché in Bill Belichick's well-worn book. The veteran quarterback's

reluctance to speak during the first week of camp, and the disclosure that he wouldn't be doing his paid radio gig with the WEEI morning boys, led some of us to wonder whether we wouldn't hear from him until the first week of October, after his four-game suspension had concluded.

But Brady did speak. Sort of.

We were hoping for something along the lines of "Roger Goodell is a boob and I can't wait to tell him to shove the Lombardi Trophy into his truck when he hands it over to me in Houston next February."

NO.

We were hoping for, "The fans need to know that their quarterback is not a cheater. I am not a cheater. And I am taking names of all those who have not stood by me during this ordeal."

NO.

We were hoping for "Jimmy G is a nice kid, but everybody knows he can't carry my shoulder pads."

NO.

We were hoping for "You need me on that wall and you're damn right I ordered the code red!"

NO.

We got Patriotspeak. Bradyspeak. Zzzzzzz.

"I've tried to just be as positive as I can be," said Brady. "I think that's kind of always been my motto. I know over the course of my career, I've been faced with different things and I've tried to overcome them the best way I could or the best way I knew how. I'll try to do the same thing.

"It's tough competition, the NFL. Every team is working

real hard this time of year and we can't take any days off. We have to go out there and try to work on something every day. Everyone has to be ready to go."

Asked about dropping his appeal, he said, "I think it's just personal. I've tried to move on from it. I try to just, like I said, focus on the positive, being here with my teammates and getting better.

"You don't want to go out and do anything but try to be a great example for your teammates. We've got a lot of competitive guys that have been out here on the practice field and I think that's where the focus needs to be.

"I have a job to do, and I try to approach it the best way I can. I've always tried to do things the same way. Every day is important to me.

"Certainly as someone who's been around here for a long time, I know I have to bring it every day. I think I just try to go out there and lead by example, try to bring it and show my teammates that I'm ready to bring it mentally and physically every day."

No surprise there. Led by quarterback Tom Brady — court-ordered to wear the Scarlet D of Deflategate — the Patriots would carry themselves publicly as if none of this over-punishment was happening. And then they would scorch the earth of Goodell's NFL America.

DAN SHAUGHNESSY • *Globe Staff*

The Patriots and Tom Brady had been at odds with NFL Commissioner Roger Goodell for nearly two years, and Brady addressed the media on Aug. 5 for the first time after dropping his appeal of the four-game "Deflategate" suspension, which became a federal case.

TIME OUT!

CARDINALS
DOLPHINS
TEXANS
BILLS
BROWNS
BENGALS
STEELERS
BILLS
SEAHAWKS
49ERS
JETS
RAMS
RAVENS
BRONCOS
JETS
DOLPHINS

9/11/16 ☞ GLENDALE, AZ
On this night, Bill Belichick earned the upper hand in the long-running referendum on which Patriot is most responsible for the team's uninterrupted NFL eminence, the canonized coach or the canonized quarterback.

No Tom Brady. No Rob Gronkowski. No starting left tackle Nate Solder. A quarterback, Jimmy Garoppolo, with no career starts. It was all no problem for His Hoodiness with 150 days to prepare for the Arizona Cardinals. His team left the desert with a 23-21 victory over the Cardinals at University of Phoenix Stadium.

The NFL schedule was released on April 14. Giving Belichick nearly five months to dissect an opponent is like giving Usain Bolt a 10-meter head start in the 100-meter dash. It's almost unfair. Belichick and Patriots offensive coordinator Josh McDaniels put that time to good use, crafting a game plan that kept their neophyte quarterback in his comfort zone and out of trouble. Garoppolo was good, finishing 24 of 33 for 264 yards with a touchdown and leading the Patriots to the winning points with a fourth-quarter drive.

BB and defensive coordinator Matt Patricia stifled an offense that averaged 30.6 points per game last season, allowing them to score 14 of their points only after Patriot turnovers gave them a short field.

Larry Fitzgerald's 100th career TD reception, an acrobatic 1-yard grab on a fade route, forced Garoppolo to play from behind for the first time all night, as the Cardinals took a 21-20 lead with 9:46 left in the fourth quarter. The pressure was on both the kid and Belichick.

Garoppolo led the Patriots back down the field for the go-ahead Stephen Gostkowski field goal with 3:44 to go. The key play on the drive was Jimmy G scrambling to buy time on third and 15 from his own 20 and then delivering a strike for 32 yards to Danny Amendola.

Then Belichick made sure it stood up.

The last time the Patriots played in this building, Belichick didn't call a timeout with the opponent on the verge of the winning points. The Seattle Seahawks threw the ball to Malcolm Butler, throwing away certain victory in Super Bowl XLIX.

This time, Belichick called a timeout with 41 seconds left when the Cardinals, out of timeouts, were rushing on the field to kick the potential game-winning 47-yard field goal. It was Belichick right again, as a bad snap forced Cardinals kicker Chandler Catanzaro to yank his kick wide left.

The Patriots might have been 9½-point underdogs in their season opener, but the wise guys in Vegas haven't figured out that Belichick is the wisest of them all.
»CHRISTOPHER L. GASPER

23-21

NE	10	0	7	6
ARI	0	7	7	7

The Patriots open the season with 18 players who were not on their 2015 roster and a fill-in QB, as Jimmy Garoppolo plays a solid game spelling the suspended Tom Brady.

CARDINALS
DOLPHINS

9/18/16 ● FOXBOROUGH

Jimmy Garoppolo was having a grand homecoming, shredding the Dolphins with surgical precision in his first start in front of the Gillette Stadium faithful. And then Kiko Alonso crashed the party. The Miami linebacker drove Garoppolo to the turf late in the first half and the Patriots quarterback suffered a shoulder injury and left the game, which the Patriots hung on to win, 31-24.

Garoppolo was nearly flawless before he went down, torching the Dolphins for 234 yards and three touchdowns as the Patriots scored 21 points on their first three drives. He finished with 18 completions on 27 attempts.

Garoppolo had the Patriots on the move when he was thumped on the team's sixth possession. Rolling to his right, he was drilled a split second after firing a 15-yard completion to rookie Malcolm Mitchell. The third-year quarterback staggered toward the sideline before dropping to a knee. He was helped off by the medical staff and headed straight to the locker room.

Enter rookie Jacoby Brissett, who finished off the drive that ended with a Stephen Gostkowski 24-yard field goal.

"We just told everybody to keep playing, keep doing what you're doing," said tight end Martellus Bennett when asked what went on when Brissett entered the huddle. "We still had to make plays and be patient. Hurry back to the huddle and give him time to make the calls. It was pretty much the same — everybody was on the same page."

Brissett hardly looked overwhelmed. He was asked to play caretaker mostly, and he did without a problem, completing 6 of 9 passes for 92 yards — including a 37-yarder to Bennett on a pump fake and twirl. Most importantly, he didn't make any glaring mistakes.

"Jacoby, he's been working for this for a long time, all the way back into the spring, all the way through training camp," said Belichick. "He's gotten a lot of reps. He did a good job [in a] pressure situation. [He] played 2½ quarters and he did a good job for us."

Brissett's most impressive drive was his first of the second half, when he went 3 for 3 on a five-play, 68-yard drive that was capped by LeGarrette Blount's 9-yard bulldozing run. The touchdown ran the hosts' lead to 31-3.

With Tom Brady and Garoppolo splitting most of the snaps during training camp, Brissett didn't get a lot of time with the starting offense, but he didn't look uncomfortable.

When he was asked how much time he's worked with the starters since arriving, Brissett said with a smile, "Enough to, you know, go out there and get a win."

»JIM McBRIDE

31-24

MIA	0	3	7	14
NE	14	10	7	0

Having led the Patriots on three straight scoring drives to start the game, Jimmy Garoppolo is sidelined when he hurts his shoulder on this tackle by Miami's Kiko Alonso.

9/22/16 ● FOXBOROUGH
Bill Belichick and the Patriots delivered yet another strong message to Roger Goodell and NFL America Thursday night. Playing without Tom Brady ... playing without Brady's backup ... playing their second game in five days ... established as underdogs on their home field ... playing with a rookie quarterback starting his first NFL game ... the Patriots humiliated the heretofore undefeated Houston Texans, 27-0, at Gillette Stadium.

Take that, Roger.

Belichick sarcastically told us in Arizona that he is a big fan of "story lines" so here goes: Rookie Jacoby Brissett (11 for 19, 103 yards, zero TDs, zero picks) played Game Management 101 and scored a touchdown on a dazzling 27-yard QB option in the first quarter; the Patriots' defense inspired memories of the 1985 Chicago Bears; Bill O'Brien and the Texans did what everybody else does when they see Belichick and the Gillette lighthouse — they got weak in the knees and wet their pants. It was downright embarrassing for a coach who worked here and should have been better prepared.

But the No. 1 story line of the night was Belichick. We keep thinking we have seen the ultimate demonstration of his greatness and then we see something that tops the last one. We thought the opening-night win at Arizona would stand as the Hoodie's favorite non-Super Bowl win, but this shocker against the Texans was even better. It was a game won by all the boring things Bill loves — special teams, defense, and mistake-free offense.

"I'm so proud of the way our guys competed," said Belichick. "A real satisfying win. The whole week the coaching staff did a tremendous job."

Leading into this game, there was no shortage of speculation on who would quarterback the Patriots. Wonderboy Jimmy Garoppolo sprained the AC joint in his throwing shoulder in the second quarter of the win over Miami and suddenly everybody had an opinion about what might unfold four days later.

Given that the Patriots opted not to sign a journeyman QB for a one-night stand, this left the team in the hands of rookie Brissett with the only backup being wide receiver Julian Edelman. Brissett had a pretty good first half. Late in the first quarter, he scampered 27 yards on a quarterback keeper to score his first NFL touchdown and give the Patriots a 10-0 lead.

Somewhere in the swamps of Jersey, the Almighty Tuna (Brissett's mentor, Bill Parcells) had to be smiling.

»DAN SHAUGHNESSY

27-0

HOU	0	0	0	0
NE	10	0	10	7

Jacoby Brissett dives into the end zone to complete a 27-yard option run that gave the Patriots a 10-0 lead over the Houston Texans in his winning debut as a starting QB.

10/2/16 ● FOXBOROUGH

Let the church bells ring, let the rejoicing begin, and let the payback tour commence. Tom Brady's four-game Deflategate suspension is finished and the Patriots are still in their customary perch atop the AFC East.

That's what matters, not Rex Ryan and the Buffalo Bills taking advantage of novice quarterback Jacoby Brissett to deliver Vociferous Rex's brand of industrial justice to Bill Belichick, handing the Hoodie the first Patriots shutout loss in the history of Gillette Stadium. Rarely has a Patriots loss, even one as distasteful as the 16-0 drubbing by the Bills, felt so insignificant.

If I told you before Brady started serving the NFL's version of hard time for soft-ish footballs that the Patriots were going to start third-string rookie Brissett for half of the games Brady missed and the team was still going to win three of four you would have taken it. Injected with sodium pentothal and stripped of his arsenal of dour, deflecting argot, Belichick would have taken it, too.

Deflategate dinged Brady's sterling reputation, but it barely put a dent in the Patriots' championship pursuit. The NFL took a shot at the Patriots and it missed.

You're not going to get much perspective and introspection on 35,000-foot thoughts like the team's positive performance during TB12's absence after a loss. The excitement over Brady's return was — unlike Ryan — muted. So was the Patriots' offense by Buffalo's defense, which seized on Brissett's limited NFL experience, his wrapped-up right thumb, and a pared-down playbook.

Brissett was just 3 of 3 for 75 yards in the first half with a crushing fumble at the Buffalo 9. He finished 17 of 27 for 205 yards.

The Patriots were down, 10-0, before they picked up their initial first down early in the second quarter. The Patriots were outgained, 251 to 98, in the first half and 58 of those yards came on one pass to Martellus Bennett.

For the game, New England sputtered to 1 of 12 on third down. But the only 12 that matters now is No. 12.

"It's going to be good to have him back," said Brady BFF Julian Edelman, who took a few snaps at QB against Buffalo. "Any time one of your best players isn't there there's something missing. We handled a lot of it well. Today we just didn't."

»CHRISTOPHER L. GASPER

16-0

BUF	7	6	3	0
NE	0	0	0	0

Kicker Stephen Gostkowski laments his missed field-goal attempt in the third quarter of the Bills' 16-0 victory, the first time the Patriots had been shut out at home since 1993.

10/9/16 ● CLEVELAND, OH

More than a year and a half later — after "11 out of 12 balls" lost pressure, Mona Lisa Vito, the Wells Report In Context, Jimmy "Hotfingers" McNally, Fanboy Judge Berman, the Ideal Gas Law, Defending The Wall, and Free Tom Brady — the Patriots finally put Deflategate behind them at FirstEnergy Stadium on the banks of Lake Erie.

Brady returned from his football Alcatraz (a sentence served alternately at the Big House in Ann Arbor and sunbathing nude in Capri), torching the poor, pitiful Cleveland Browns, 33-13, in front of thousands of road trippers with Boston accents on an absolutely perfect football Sunday. Brady completed 28 of 40 passes for a Ted Williams-esque 406 yards, completed three touchdown passes to Martellus Bennett, and was not intercepted.

"I want to do the best job I can for the city, for all of New England, for my teammates and for my family," said Brady. "You have to make certain choices in life to play this game. ... I love running out in front of 20,000 fans that are cheering for us when 50,000 are against us. It's just fun to run out and play."

Asked how it felt to have Deflategate behind him, Brady went into Fort Foxborough mode and said, "I was just thinking about today and what I had to do."

Was he inspired by "perceived slights," i.e. the slings and arrows of the commissioner, the Wells Report, and his highly publicized punishment?

"This isn't a time for me to reflect," he answered. "I'm happy we won today. I'm happy we win every time we play. I have a job to do and there's no point in looking back whether we won Super Bowls, or lost championship games, or the last four weeks. None of it matters. Just go out and do the best I can do every week."

One of the highlights for road-tripping Patriot Nation came late in the third quarter when Brady scrambled to his right and chugged 4 yards to the sideline for a relatively meaningless first down. Brady was hit pretty hard at the end of the play, but bounced up and defiantly gave the "first down" signal as much of the Patriot-garbed crowd roared its approval.

"I don't run much so when I do, I was a little excited," he said.

"I think we've got the best fans in the world," added Brady. "They showed up today and it was great to hear them."

»DAN SHAUGHNESSY

33-13

NE	16	7	7	3
CLE	7	0	0	6

After a third-quarter scramble, Tom Brady makes a joyous first-down signal. Brady finally made his season debut in Cleveland, where he was reunited with rampaging Rob Gronkowski.

10/16/16 ● FOXBOROUGH

Tom Brady's return to Gillette Stadium felt like a football family reunion. Two of his sisters, Nancy and Julie, and sons Jack and Benjamin were in attendance to see his first home game after four games as the NFL's air pressure prisoner. Brady also had more than 66,000 extended family members welcoming him home.

The golden boy QB didn't disappoint. He went 29 of 35 for 376 yards and three touchdowns in a 35-17 victory over the Cincinnati Bengals.

It's clear the Deflategate saga has only strengthened the bond between Brady and the fan base. He is both a matinee idol and a martyr. He has come to embody not only the unyielding excellence of the Patriots but their perceived persecution for said excellence.

It had been exactly nine months since Brady played a game at Gillette. The last time he set foot on the field for game action was Jan. 16, a 27-20 playoff victory over the Kansas City Chiefs.

Before the Patriots took the field, a TB12 tribute video was played and then the video board cut to Troy Brown opening the locker room door to reveal Brady leading the team out. The crowd erupted. It grew more boisterous when Brady ran through the inflatable tunnel the team uses to take the field.

It was like those games the Patriots won with Jimmy Garoppolo and Jacoby Brissett at quarterback never happened.

But the Bengals had no intention of playing pliant football foils for Brady's welcome-home party, especially in the early going. Brady was forced to hold the ball, move off the spot, and search for open receivers. He finally found James White in the end zone with 1:01 left in the first half to give New England a 10-7 halftime lead.

Former TB12 target Brandon LaFell caught a 5-yard touchdown pass on the first possession of the second half to give Cincy a 14-10 lead. But then Cincinnati succumbed to a blitz from Dont'a Hightower and its own self-destructive nature. After Andy Dalton was sacked for a safety, Brady completed seven of his next eight passes — six of them to Martellus Bennett or Rob Gronkowski — on two touchdown drives.

On the Patriots' final four drives, Brady guided them to four scores (touchdown, touchdown, field goal, touchdown). He finished the second half 17 of 19 for 240 yards and two TDs. Twice, he connected with Gronk for 38-yard gains to set up scores. The second 38-yarder, a floater under pressure with 4:33 left in the third quarter, was the 5,000th completion of Brady's illustrious career.

»CHRISTOPHER L. GASPER

35-17

CIN	0	7	7	3
NE	3	7	15	10

Fans in the south end-zone seats at Gillette Stadium make sure Tom Brady knows that he was missed, and he responds to their tribute by going 29 for 35 with three touchdown passes.

10/23/16 ● PITTSBURGH, PA
The Patriots defense doesn't allow a lot of points. But it does allow for a lot of backhanded compliments and varying views on just how good the unit is.

They're statistically impressive but aesthetically adequate. They leave you wanting more. None of that changed in the team's 27-16 victory over the Ben Roethlisberger-less Steelers at Heinz Field. The defense did its job, but it also left you wondering how Pittsburgh backup quarterback Landry Jones could throw for nearly 300 yards and the Steelers could be allowed to hang around long past their bedtime.

No one remembers that Pittsburgh still had dynamic running back Le'Veon Bell (21 rushes for 81 yards and 10 receptions for 68 yards) and all-world wide receiver Antonio Brown (seven catches for 106 yards) at its disposal.

"I feel like every year it's something. We'll never be just, 'You're a good defensive team.' Nobody will say that to us," said safety Devin McCourty. "So, we don't care. Whatever we are in points allowed we know that's what's important. We know that is what the game comes down to."

There was a five-drive stretch in this game where the Steelers got the ball in their territory and drove to the Patriots' 14, 24, 14, 28, and 26. The results were touchdown, missed field goal, field goal, field goal, and field goal. Belichick always says sacks are overrated, but the Patriots didn't get Jones to the ground once.

On the other hand, the Patriots held the Steelers to 5 of 16 on third down and allowed one touchdown in four red-zone trips. The Patriots defense bailed out the offense after Chris Hogan fumbled on New England's first offensive snap of the game. Malcolm Butler made a brilliant end-zone interception on a pass intended for Brown, setting up the Patriots' first score.

In the fourth quarter with the Patriots leading 27-16, Julian Edelman fumbled a punt and put the defibrillator paddles on Pittsburgh, which recovered at the Patriots' 43 with 10:37 left. The defense only allowed 7 yards. Steelers coach Mike Tomlin foolishly elected to have Chris Boswell attempt a 54-yard field goal in a stadium that is a graveyard for field-goal kickers. The kick missed.

This was a theme for the Steelers. They were willing accomplices in their own demise. They missed two field goals, squandered turnover opportunities, committed false-start penalties, and showed situational ignorance instead of situational awareness. Cue the calliope.

»CHRISTOPHER L. GASPER

27-16

NE	7	7	6	7
PIT	0	10	3	3

Malcolm Butler seizes the moment, snagging an end-zone pass intended for Antonio Brown to keep the Steelers from scoring after a rare Patriots' turnover in the first quarter.

10/30/16 ● ORCHARD PARK, NY
The flavor of the day in Buffalo on this October Sunday: Salty.

The Bills were in no mood to congratulate Rob Gronkowski after the Patriots' tight end broke Stanley Morgan's team record for career touchdowns, scoring his 69th in the Patriots' 41-25 win.

"He uses his body well, but he's got Tom Brady," Bills safety Corey Graham said. "I mean, Tom Brady's Tom Brady."

"I'm more impressed with [Martellus] Bennett than Gronk," Bills linebacker Zach Brown added. "When Tom Brady wasn't here, you didn't hear [Gronkowski]. But when Tom Brady comes back he knows where to place it, how to place it, and he uses Gronk's size to his advantage."

We'll excuse the Bills for being a little bitter. It couldn't have been fun to watch Gronkowski and the Patriots march up and down the field, scoring points on seven of nine drives before Brady was mercifully lifted from the game with 4:29 remaining.

Gronkowski dominated once again, catching five passes for 109 yards and a 53-yard touchdown in the second quarter that broke open a close game. And he

did it in front of a few dozen close family and friends in his hometown of Buffalo.

Gronkowski received a call from Morgan, who played with the Patriots from 1977-89, after the game. Morgan scored his 68 touchdowns in 180 career games. Gronkowski has 69 TDs in just 85 regular-season games.

"Definitely an honor," Gronkowski said. "He said congratulations, and it was pretty cool."

"He makes it easy on anybody throwing him the ball," Brady said of Gronk in Week 7. "He's got great length, and catch radius, and speed and quickness for his size. He can run the whole route tree, so he's just a great target."

We saw Gronk's great hands when he snatched a back-shoulder throw out of the air at the last second. We saw his power when he bulldozed through several defenders on the same catch, turning it into a 31-yard gain.

We saw his nimble feet, when he tapped his toes along the sideline for an 18-yard catch in the third quarter.

"That was something special that you don't expect from Gronk," Bennett said. "That was nice."

In addition to setting the Patriots' all-time touchdown record, Gronkowski became the 14th tight end in NFL history with 6,000 career receiving yards. He has 23 100-yard games, third most by a tight end in NFL history. And the Brady-Gronk connection has produced 67 touchdowns, tied with Peyton Manning and Reggie Wayne for the sixth-most by any duo in NFL history.
»BEN VOLIN

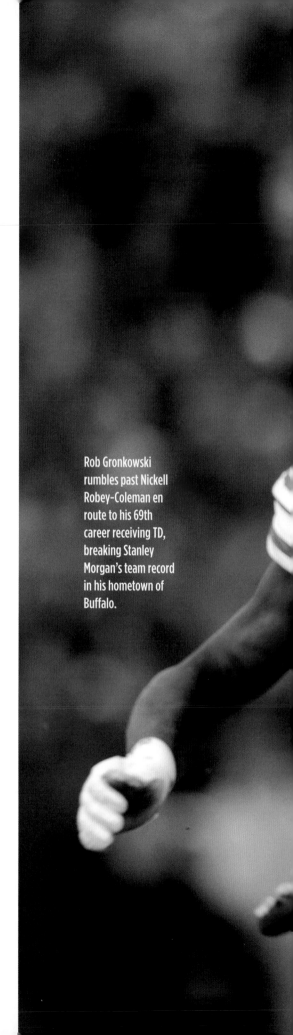

Rob Gronkowski rumbles past Nickell Robey-Coleman en route to his 69th career receiving TD, breaking Stanley Morgan's team record in his hometown of Buffalo.

41-25

NE	14	10	14	3
BUF	3	7	7	8

11/13/16 • FOXBOROUGH

The group "Go West" had a wistful pop song called "King of Wishful Thinking." Seahawks coach Pete Carroll is the King of Overthinking against the Patriots. He proved that again last night with his brain stuck buffering in crunch time while he tried to match wits with Bill Belichick. Pumped and Jacked Pete made all the wrong moves once again against the Patriots. It didn't matter this time.

Carroll has instilled his team with so much resolve, resilience, and relentlessness that they overcame his questionable late-game strategy to hand the Patriots a 31-24 loss at Gillette Stadium. The sequel to Super Bowl XLIX lived up to the hype. The NFL wishes its prime-time product always came replete with this much cachet, quality football, and entertainment value.

Seattle won a see-saw affair that saw five lead changes in the second half, as the Seahawks handed the Patriots their first loss since Tom Brady returned from his suspension, and a sobering reminder that their defense is vulnerable.

The upshot is that both of these teams are Super Bowl-caliber,

but only one of these coaches has a doctorate degree in in-game strategy. Maligned for his disastrous decision to throw the ball from the 1-yard line in Super Bowl XLIX, Carroll again made some head-scratching decisions.

After Russell Wilson threw his third touchdown pass of the game — a steely-eyed 15-yarder on third down to Doug Baldwin — to put the Seahawks up, 31-24, with 4:24 to go, Carroll foolishly elected to go for a 2-point conversion instead of kicking the extra point to go up 8.

Seattle had the extra point blocked on its first TD.

Belichick was caught by the NBC cameras asking the same question as the rest of us, "Why is he going for 2?"

"Yeah, we wanted to see if we could put it out of reach and make it a two-score deal," said Carroll. Of course, the conversion failed, which meant the Patriots only had to march down the field and score a touchdown and kick the extra point to tie.

It all worked out in Carroll's favor when on fourth and goal from the 1, the Patriots elected to throw a fade to Rob Gronkowski. After Gronk and Seattle's Kam Chancellor tussled for position like it was an offensive rebound, the ball harmlessly hit the turf and Carroll was off the hook.

The former Patriots coach didn't have to explain away how he botched another game against Belichick and the Patriots. Carroll's questionable decision-making became a footnote to a great night of football in Foxborough.

»CHRISTOPHER L. GASPER

31-24

SEA	6	13	3	9
NE	7	7	7	3

Rob Gronkowski grimaces as he absorbs a second-quarter hit from Seattle safety Earl Thomas. Gronkowski underwent season-ending back surgery 2 1/2 weeks later.

11/20/16 ● SANTA CLARA, CA
Tommy Brady. Homecoming King.

The New England Patriots trumped the moribund San Francisco 49ers, 30-17, at Levi's Stadium and Brady — playing in front of family, friends, and Patriot Nation West for the first time in his 17-year career — led the way with 280 yards of completions, including four touchdown passes.

It was a sweet Sunday for the Patriot icon as he finally had a chance to show the locals what they missed when they passed on him (as did every other team for 5½ rounds) at the 2000 NFL Draft.

We watched three quarters of slippery, grinding football in a steady rain before the Patriots secured their victory with a pair of quick-strike touchdowns early in the fourth. With just over nine minutes left, a large portion of the Niners "home" crowd toasted QB12 with chants of "Bra-dy, Bra-dy."

As the clocked ticked down toward 0:00, the sun broke through and a giant rainbow settled over the 49ers' massive new stadium. Such are the powers of Tommy Brady. He can avoid the rush, throw on the run, make the rain stop, and the sun shine.

He is "Tommy" here. Never Tom. That's what his family and friends call him.

Though Brady is increasingly reserved with the media, he didn't dismiss or minimize how much it meant to him to play and win in San Francisco. He grew up cheering for the Joe Montana 49ers at Candlestick Park and the entire Brady clan was wounded when San Francisco passed on him in favor of the immortal Giovanni Carmazzi (zero NFL snaps) in 2000.

Brady's assessment of his Homecoming in front of thousands of fans wearing Patriot Brady jerseys?

"It was very cool," he said. "It doesn't get any better than that. To have a first chance to be back was very special. I felt it during pregame warm-ups and I kept it until the last play of the game ... To see [former Niners fullback] Tom Rathman before the game, and Dwight Clark and Joe Montana, to see them at halftime, it was a pretty great day for me."

Sunday's weather made life difficult for every player on both sides, but Brady wasn't complaining. He made some of his best plays late in the third quarter when it was especially sloppy.

"I prefer 72 and sunny, but I know the Bay Area hasn't had rain in a long time," said Brady. "We need rain out here, that's what my parents said and I'm very happy about that."

OK, then. Done. Tommy Brady finally played and won in San Francisco. A mid-November Super Bowl for the greatest quarterback of all time.

»DAN SHAUGHNESSY

30-17

NE	6	7	0	17
SF	3	7	0	7

Tom Brady, who grew in nearby San Mateo, Calif., warms up for his "homecoming" game at Levi's Stadium in Santa Clara against his boyhood heroes, the San Francisco 49ers.

CARDINALS
DOLPHINS
TEXANS
BILLS
BROWNS
BENGALS
STEELERS
BILLS
SEAHAWKS
49ERS
JETS
RAMS
RAVENS
BRONCOS
JETS
DOLPHINS

11/27/16 ● E. RUTHERFORD, NJ
You have seen this game one million times. Maybe two million.

The Patriots struggle. The other team plays over its head. It looks like we might witness an upset loss for the team from Fort Foxborough. And then all the usual elements emerge and the Patriots cut out the hearts of their rivals. Tom Brady plays cool, flawless football down the stretch, the Patriots wait for the other guys to step on banana peels, and New England walks out of another enemy stadium with a hard-fought victory.

"It says a lot about our team," Bill Belichick said after the Patriots trumped the Jets, 22-17, at MetLife Stadium. "Their resiliency and mental toughness ... You battle it out for 59 minutes and it comes down to one or two plays."

The Patriots beat you because they are smarter and tougher. They never take the apple. If you are from Buffalo, Miami, or the Meadowlands, they take away your will to live. They make the plays when the plays need to be made and they wait for you to tie your shoelaces together, which you inevitably will do. It is all so predictable.

"We didn't play as well as we wanted to," Brady said after connecting with Malcolm Mitchell for the winning touchdown pass (in front of Darrelle Revis, of course) with less than two minutes left. "We made the plays when we needed to."

Rob Gronkowski, who already had a chest injury, suffered a back injury and left in the first quarter. Stephen Gostkowski missed a 39-yard field goal attempt. Malcolm Butler was beaten on a pair of touchdown passes. The Patriots did not take their first lead against the last-place Jets (3-8) until the middle of the third quarter. With seven minutes to play, the Patriots trailed, 17-16, and the Jets had the football.

That's when the Patriots became the Patriots and the Jets became the Jets. They had a block in the back on the kickoff. Their Harvard quarterback was tagged with a dumbbell intentional grounding. They took no time off the clock, punted away the ball, and played coverage, allowing Brady to surgically dissect them.

The Patriots had to convert a fourth-and-4 from the Jets' 37 to keep their hopes alive. No problem. Brady connected with James White in the right flat and White got the nose of the football to the Jets' 33.

That's why winners win and why Jets lose. And if you are a New England Patriots fan, it's always a good day when the Jets lose.

»DAN SHAUGHNESSY

22-17

NE	0	10	3	9
NYJ	3	7	0	7

Malcolm Mitchell beats former Patriot Darrelle Revis (24) for a 4-yard touchdown pass in the second quarter. Mitchell later added the game-winning TD on an 8-yard reception.

CARDINALS
DOLPHINS
TEXANS
BILLS
BROWNS
BENGALS
STEELERS
BILLS
SEAHAWKS
49ERS
JETS
RAMS
RAVENS
BRONCOS
JETS
DOLPHINS

12/4/16 ● FOXBOROUGH
The wide-eyed kid quarterback who put his hands to his head in disbelief after the Patriots won their first Super Bowl way back in February 2002 is long gone, replaced by a grizzled all-time great whose mastery of the position and competitive drive never get old.

No NFL record with his name on it defines the essence of Tom Brady more than the one he established against the Los Angeles Rams at Gillette Stadium for most wins by a quarterback. Since the moment he got his opportunity in 2001, Brady has found a way to win at the most high-pressure and high-profile position in North American sports.

The Patriots' 26-10 victory over the Rams was the 201st time Brady has quarterbacked the Patriots to victory, including the postseason. He is 201-61 in his career. No other NFL quarterback has ever reached a record of 140 games above .500. You can argue whether wins should be ascribed to quarterbacks like baseball pitchers, but as long as they are, all other quarterback stats are for losers. Brady is the

consummate winner.

If you needed any reminder of how grateful the Foxborough Faithful should be to the scorekeeper in the sky for Brady's prolonged brilliance, it was on display at Gillette Stadium as more than 40 of Brady's former teammates from the '01 team returned to celebrate the 15-year anniversary of that team.

While his ex-teammates were basking in the glow of history, the 39-year-old Brady was out on the field still making it for the 10-2 Patriots.

"Quite frankly, it's unreal," said Patriots receiver and Brady confidant Julian Edelman. "It just shows you that is what separates him from the other guys. You look at all the other greats, I mean when they're at this age they don't look like him, not even close."

While this was a day to revel in history and memories, it wasn't a game that deserved any space in the memory banks.

The stark dichotomy between a quarterback with 201 wins and a rookie QB searching for his first NFL win robbed this contest of any competitiveness. Rams quarterback and 2016 No. 1 overall pick Jared Goff was 7 years old when Brady directed the Patriots to victory in Super Bowl XXXVI.

This victory for Brady over the Rams lacked any of the drama and suspense of that one. No final-drive heroics required. It was rudimentary. LA was outgained, 230-25, in the first half and registered one first down. The Rams couldn't get beyond their own 36 until the second half and finished the game 1 for 12 on third down.

»CHRISTOPHER L. GASPER

26-10

LA	0	0	3	7
NE	7	10	6	3

Tom Brady (12) watches as Chris Hogan gathers in his pass for a score in the second quarter of Brady's 201st victory, snapping a tie with Peyton Manning for career wins by a QB.

12/12/16 ● FOXBOROUGH
Ravens coach John Harbaugh had the No. 1 defense in the NFL, in both points and yards allowed. But when it came to crunch time in this Monday night contest, he had no faith in being able to stop Tom Brady and the Patriots offense.

Trailing by 7 points with 2:03 left and holding two timeouts, Harbaugh opted for an onside kick instead of kicking deep. The Patriots recovered, and four plays later closed out a 30-23 win in what may have been their most difficult challenge left this regular season.

And it's hard to blame Harbaugh for deciding to onside kick. The Patriots offense was rolling, and not even the Ravens' top-ranked defense could slow it down.

"Ravens are a good team. They're tough, they do a lot of things well," Bill Belichick said. "We just did a few things a little better tonight. We'll take it."

December is finals time across New England, and the Patriots offense aced its big test.

No Rob Gronkowski? No problem.

The Ravens had their worst statistical game of the season, in points, yards, and on third down.

The Ravens entered the game allowing just 17.3 points and 296.1 yards per game, but the Patriots took a blowtorch to those numbers. They gained 496 total yards, their second-highest total of the season, including 406 passing yards for Brady. The Patriots also converted 8 of 16 third downs against a Ravens defense that had been No. 1 in the NFL at 33 percent.

And the Patriots should've had at least 3 more points, if not 7 more, had Brady not thrown a terrible end-zone interception in the second quarter.

"There were some plays I wish we all would've had back. They're a competitive team, they force you into some errors," said Brady, whose 406 yards tied his season high, set at Cleveland in Week 5. "But it was great to finish the game with the ball in our hands."

Four receivers stepped up with at least 70 yards — Chris Hogan (129), James White (81), Julian Edelman (73), and Martellus Bennett (70). LeGarrette Blount added 72 yards on the ground.

And while Edelman was still Brady's favorite receiver — his 15 targets were more than double the next-highest player (Hogan with seven) — the Patriots displayed great depth. Seven players caught a pass, three guys caught a touchdown, and the Patriots uncorked an impressive big-play ability, hitting six plays of at least 27 yards.

"You play at home in December on Monday night against a great defense, it was important for us to come out and play well," Brady said. "Big win for us."

»BEN VOLIN

30-23

BAL	0	3	14	6
NE	9	7	7	7

Linebacker Shea McClellin vaults over the Ravens' offensive line to block a field-goal attempt by Justin Tucker, the first missed FG of the season by the Baltimore kicker.

CARDINALS
DOLPHINS
TEXANS
BILLS
BROWNS
BENGALS
STEELERS
BILLS
SEAHAWKS
49ERS
JETS
RAMS
RAVENS
BRONCOS
JETS
DOLPHINS

12/18/16 ● DENVER, CO

It must be December in the AFC. Chestnuts are roasting on open fires and Tomato Cans are falling down in front of the sons of Bill Belichick.

This was yet another hat and T-shirt game for the New England Patriots. Playing one of their best games of the season, the Patriots Trumped the defending Super Bowl champion Denver Broncos, 16-3, at Mile High, winning the AFC East for the eighth consecutive season and the 13th time in the last 14 years. The Patriots are 14-2 in AFC East titles since Tom Brady took over at quarterback in 2001.

For the Patriots, winning the AFC East has become like signing up for Facebook or getting a letter of acceptance from the University of Phoenix. It's the professional sports version of a youth soccer participation trophy. All the Patriots have to do to win is show up, play their traditional tight game, and wait for the other guys to make mistakes.

The chorus line of dunce coaches (Cam Cameron?) and bum quarterbacks (Thad Lewis?) populating the AFC East in this century stretches from Orchard Park to Miami Gardens

with an annual stop at Exit 16W off the Jersey Turnpike. And the beneficiaries of this abject ineptitude are your New England Patriots — a team that never, ever takes a year off. The Patriots' annual mission is to win the division, qualify for a bye, then secure home field for the duration of the playoffs. They do this with historic efficiency.

The Patriots didn't do anything spectacular in this game, but it's been really hard to win in Denver, and any victory at Mile High is to be coveted. Brady was 2-7 in the Bronco corral before the victory.

"It was no masterpiece, but it was what it needed to be," said Belichick.

New England led, 10-3 at halftime. It felt like 73-0. The Patriots' one and only touchdown of the day came on a 1-yard run by LeGarrette Blount. The Patriots fumbled twice on their only TD drive, but naturally recovered both drops.

The Patriots controlled the entire second half. The Broncos have one of the worst offensive lines in football and rushed for only 58 yards. They turned the ball over three times.

When it was over, the Patriots were greeted in their locker room with hats that read "champions" and T-shirts with "Hold down the East" inscribed on the front.

Last year, the Patriots didn't play to win in Miami in their final game and it cost them home field in the playoffs. That's not going to happen this year. They are going to clinch everything, then they will only have to win twice in Foxborough to make it to their seventh Super Bowl with Belichick and Brady.

Seven Super Bowls. Six straight AFC title games. Eight straight division championships. Enjoy. These are the good old days.

»DAN SHAUGHNESSY

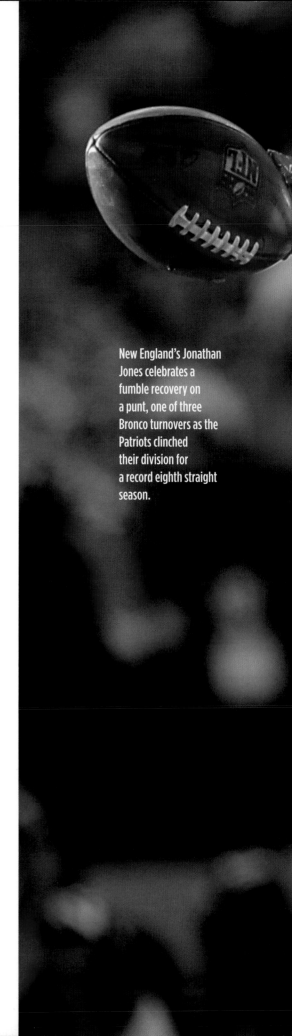

New England's Jonathan Jones celebrates a fumble recovery on a punt, one of three Bronco turnovers as the Patriots clinched their division for a record eighth straight season.

16-3

NE	3	7	3	3
DEN	3	0	0	0

12/24/16 ● FOXBOROUGH

Hey Santa, you skip Matt Lengel's house, Tom Brady's got your back.

Brady delivered the perfect present in the form of an 18-yard touchdown pass to Lengel in the second quarter of New England's 41-3, Christmas Eve day victory over the Jets at Gillette Stadium.

There's nothing Lengel's going to find under the tree that's going to beat that.

It was the first career touchdown, on his first career reception, on his first career target, for Lengel, who had a cup of coffee at Parsons Field before Northeastern shuttered its football program in 2009.

"It's No. 1 all-time on the present list," said Lengel. "And my birthday's on Dec. 27th, so it's No. 1 on both lists."

Lengel's touchdown was part of a 27-point first-half New England blitz as the Patriots took advantage of three turnovers to deliver the early knockout.

Jets quarterback Bryce Petty's Gillette Stadium debut was shortlived. He went 0 for 3 with an interception before leaving with a shoulder injury. His replacement, Ryan Fitzpatrick,

didn't fare much better, completing 8 of 21 for 136 yards and a pair of interceptions.

Brady, meanwhile, was his efficient self. He completed 17 of 27 passes for 214 yards, 3 TDs, and zero interceptions before giving way to Jimmy Garoppolo late in the third quarter.

Brady didn't have to do a ton of heavy lifting because the Patriots stuck with a balanced approach and ground out 114 yards on 40 carries.

It wasn't pretty but it was pretty effective at killing the clock and crushing the Jets' spirits. Just when the Jets thought they had made a stand, the Patriots would convert on third down (11 of 18).

LeGarrette Blount churned out 50 yards on 20 carries, collecting his 16th and 17th touchdowns of the season. Dion Lewis spun and twisted his way to 52 yards on 16 carries.

Lengel's moment was the signature play of the day and he was mobbed by his teammates after making the catch. Not a soul in the stadium thought Lengel would be on the receiving end of the pass — except for one.

"I saw where the safeties were and I took off on my route and I thought, 'I think I might get this,'" said Lengel. " So I just tried to do everything necessary in my route to make sure I got open for Tom and glad I could come through for my team there."

Brady acknowledged he wasn't looking Lengel's way immediately.

"I'm not going to say he was the first option," Brady said with a grin. "But it was pretty cool."

»JIM McBRIDE

41-3

NYJ	0	0	0	3
NE	10	17	7	7

Backup tight end Matt Lengel makes a tumbling, 18-yard touchdown catch of a Tom Brady pass – his first NFL reception – in the second quarter as the Patriots went on to rout the Jets.

CARDINALS
DOLPHINS
TEXANS
BILLS
BROWNS
BENGALS
STEELERS
BILLS
SEAHAWKS
49ERS
JETS
RAMS
RAVENS
BRONCOS
JETS
DOLPHINS

1/1/17 ● MIAMI GARDENS, FL
This brand new year is working out pretty well for Tom Brady.

The veteran quarterback's Happy New Year got off to a near-perfect start at Hard Rock Stadium when he threw three more touchdown passes in a 35-14 rout of the Miami Dolphins. The victory avenged New England's silly and costly season-ending loss to the Fish last January and completed Brady's résumé for his 15th full season as New England's starting quarterback.

Let the record show that in the controversial campaign in which Brady was forced to serve a commissioner-mandated/court-upheld, four-game suspension, QB12 came back with a vengeance. He led the Patriots to 11 wins in 12 games, throwing 28 touchdown passes with only two interceptions. We could recite his ridiculous pinball numbers all day long, so here's another one: Brady threw an NFL-record 254 passes on the road this year with zero interceptions.

With the Patriots leading, 27-14, and eight minutes left on the clock, the snowbirds and New England transplants at Hard Rock chanted, "M-V-P, M-V-P" as Brady

lined up behind center for the Patriots' final touchdown drive. This is not something you hear for a visiting player at many stadiums, arenas, or ballparks. I think some of the local fans actually joined the chorus. It's like the tired old Greatest of All Time argument. Even down here, they know that Brady's The One.

Brady and coach Bill Belichick — the Bill Russell and Red Auerbach of this century — were in generous moods after the holiday festival in southern Florida. The Hoodie feted his squad as a "very physically and mentally tough team, no question," while Brady called Dante Scarnecchia "the best offensive line coach in the NFL," and repeatedly reminded us that "we worked pretty hard to get to this position."

It is an enviable perch. Going a perfect 8-0 on the road, the Patriots are 14-2, secure in the knowledge that they get a week off before the playoffs. This is the sixth time in the Brady-Belichick era that the Patriots have earned the top seed, and they have made it to the Super Bowl in four of the previous five instances.

Brady never says much about what the Deflategate fallout has been like for him personally, but the whole experience had to hurt. By any measurement, it's clear Brady took the fall for Belichick's Spygate prior and the Robert Kraft-fueled Deflategate intransigence that triggered unreasonable sanctions from commissioner of football. The only thing Brady could do was suffer in silence and then come back and play better than ever. And that he has done.

»DAN SHAUGHNESSY

35-14

NE	14	6	7	8
MIA	0	7	7	0

Patriots linebacker Shea McClellin dodges the diving tackle attempt of Dolphin QB Matt Moore (8) after McClellin scooped up a Miami fumble in the fourth quarter.

FACTS AND FIGU

'PERFECTION IS NOT ATTAINABLE. BUT IF WE CHASE PERFECTION, WE CAN CATCH EXCELLENCE.'

VINCE LOMBARDI

BY JOHN POWERS / Globe Staff

In the National Football League each decade has its dynasty — the Packers in the '60s, the Steelers in the '70s, the 49ers in the '80s, and the Cowboys in the '90s. But what the Patriots, now well into their second decade of dominance, have achieved is unique. » It's not only their five Super Bowl titles and seven appearances since 2001, it's also the consistency of their excellence. Sixteen consecutive winning seasons and 14 AFC East divisional crowns, the last eight in a row. A record six consecutive appearances in the conference championship game. » What makes New England unique is its year-to-year stability under the same ownership. The same coach since 2000, the same quarterback since 2001 (both destined for the Hall of Fame), the same offensive and defensive coordinators since 2012. And the same philosophy based around planning, preparation, and production. » The players change from season to season in Foxborough but little else does, including the lofty expectations. "How do they keep doing this?," wondered Steve Mariucci, who coached the 49ers and Lions. "It's not supposed to work out that way. The league tries to create parity and make the bad teams better via the draft, first picks off the waiver wire — all those reasons that help the poor teams. And you know what? The Patriots just stay on top and stay on top."

SUPER

XX

46-10

CHI	13	10	21	2
NE	3	0	0	7

The wild-card Patriots reached their first Super Bowl by winning three road playoff games, capped by their 31-14, "Squish the Fish" victory over the Dolphins for the AFC title. The magical run was ended disastrously by the 15-1 Bears, who boasted one of the dominant defenses in NFL history. Chicago manhandled the Pats, recording as many sacks (7, including this one of Pats' QB Steve Grogan by Otis Wilson) as rushing yards allowed (7 yards on 11 carries).

BOWLS

The Patriots were mostly held in check by a Green Bay defense that sacked Drew Bledsoe (11) five times and picked off four of his passes. Brett Favre threw for two scores and ran for another as the Packers built a 27-14 halftime lead. New England closed to within 27-21 late in the third quarter on a Curtis Martin touchdown run, but game MVP Desmond Howard returned the ensuing kickoff 99 yards to dash the Patriots' comeback hopes.

35-21

GB	10	17	8	0
NE	14	0	7	0

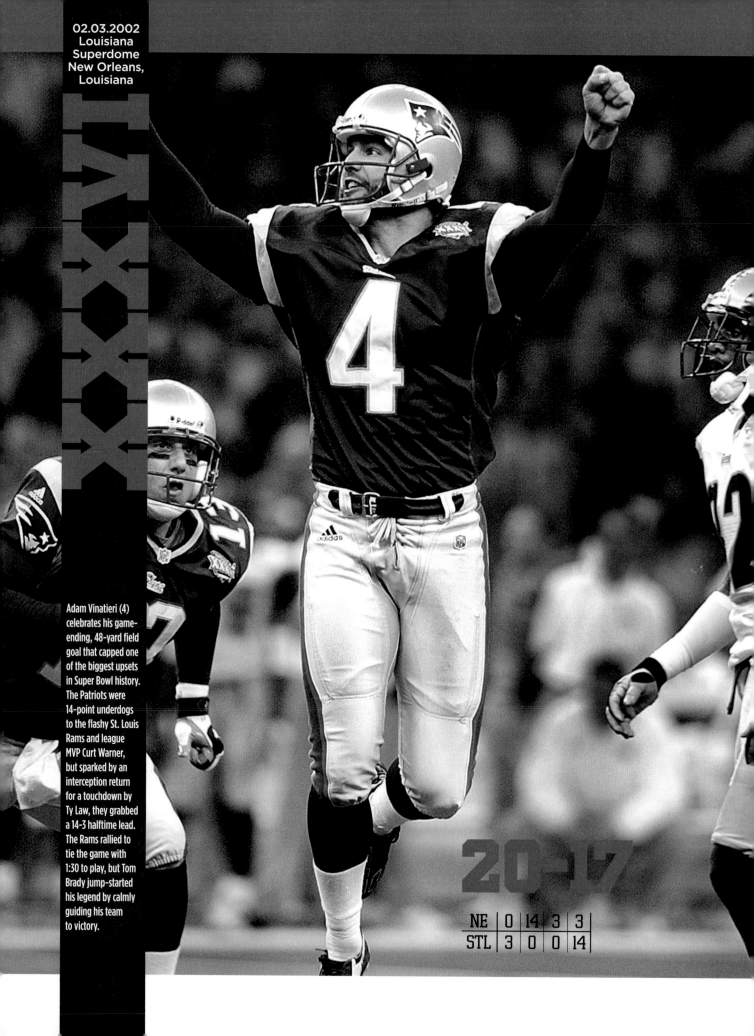

02.03.2002
Louisiana
Superdome
New Orleans,
Louisiana

XXXVI

Adam Vinatieri (4) celebrates his game-ending, 48-yard field goal that capped one of the biggest upsets in Super Bowl history. The Patriots were 14-point underdogs to the flashy St. Louis Rams and league MVP Curt Warner, but sparked by an interception return for a touchdown by Ty Law, they grabbed a 14-3 halftime lead. The Rams rallied to tie the game with 1:30 to play, but Tom Brady jump-started his legend by calmly guiding his team to victory.

2002

NE	0	14	3	3
STL	3	0	0	14

32-29

NE	0	14	0	18
CAR	0	10	0	19

The Patriots returned to the Super Bowl two years later as 6-point favorites after a 14-2 regular season. In a wild fourth quarter that featured 37 points scored, the Carolina Panthers tied the game at 29 with 1:08 to play on Jake Delhomme's third TD pass. Tom Brady again ruled the final minute, hitting 4 of 5 passes for 47 yards to set up Adam Vinatieri's 41-yard winning kick and leave safety Rodney Harrison basking in celebratory confetti.

XXXIX

24-21

NE	0	7	7	10
PHI	0	7	7	7

After another 14-2 regular season, the Patriots joined the Dallas Cowboys as the only two franchises to win three Super Bowls in four years. For the first time, the Super Bowl was tied entering the final quarter, but Tom Brady (12) drove the Patriots 66 yards to a touchdown, then to a field goal. The Eagles closed within three points, but their hopes evaporated when Rodney Harrison picked off Donovan McNabb's desperate pass, one of four Philadelphia turnovers.

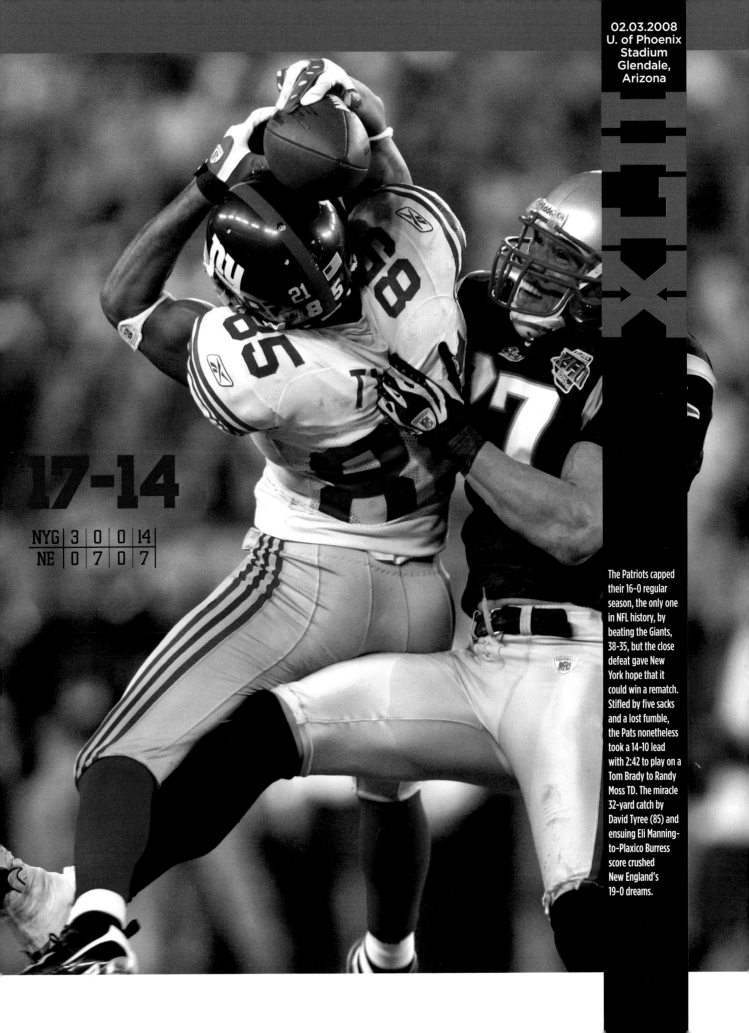

XLII

17-14

| NYG | 3 | 0 | 0 | 14 |
| NE | 0 | 7 | 0 | 7 |

The Patriots capped their 16-0 regular season, the only one in NFL history, by beating the Giants, 38-35, but the close defeat gave New York hope that it could win a rematch. Stifled by five sacks and a lost fumble, the Pats nonetheless took a 14-10 lead with 2:42 to play on a Tom Brady to Randy Moss TD. The miracle 32-yard catch by David Tyree (85) and ensuing Eli Manning-to-Plaxico Burress score crushed New England's 19-0 dreams.

02.05.2012
Lucas Oil
Stadium
Indianapolis,
Indiana

XLVI

21-17

NYG	9	0	6	6
NE	0	10	7	0

The 13-3 Patriots edged Baltimore, 23-20, for the AFC title to set up a rematch with the 9-7 New York Giants and Eli Manning. New England led, 17-9, after Tom Brady hit Aaron Hernandez for a 12-yard score, but the Giants scored the game's final 12 points on two field goals and Ahmad Bradshaw's 6-yard run with 57 seconds left. The final drive was aided by a dramatic catch, by Mario Manningham, and a crucial drop by the Patriots' Wes Welker three plays earlier.

XLIX

28-24

| NE | 0 | 14 | 0 | 14 |
| SEA | 0 | 14 | 10 | 0 |

Malcolm Butler (21) instantly entered Boston sports lore when he jumped the Seahawks' goal-line route for an interception of Russell Wilson that saved the Patriots' 28-24 victory over Seattle with 20 seconds to play. Tom Brady, who completed a Super Bowl-record 37 passes for four TDs, was the MVP for a third time as the Pats rallied from 10 points down in the final quarter. Julian Edelman tallied the game's final points on a 3-yard touchdown catch with 2:02 to play.

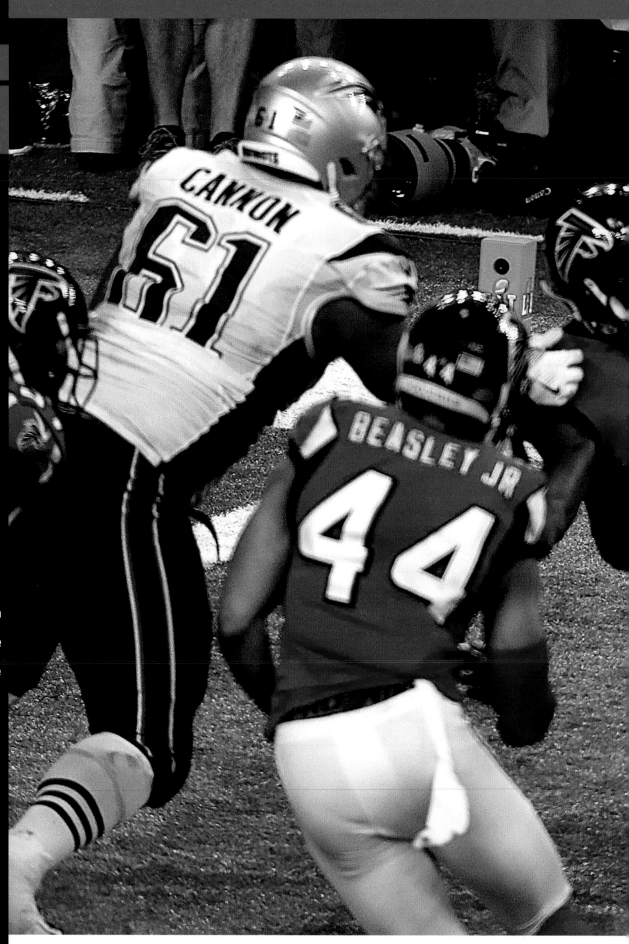

Patriots running back James White employs a stiff arm to fend off Atlanta linebacker Deion Jones (45) and right tackle Marcus Cannon leads the blocking as the Patriots complete their comeback from a 28-3 deficit to score the game-winning touchdown in the first overtime game in Super Bowl history. (Next page) Afterward, quarterback Tom Brady shared a moment with team owner Robert Kraft, whose franchise has won five titles in 16 seasons.

34-28

NE	0	3	6	19	6
ATL	0	21	7	0	0

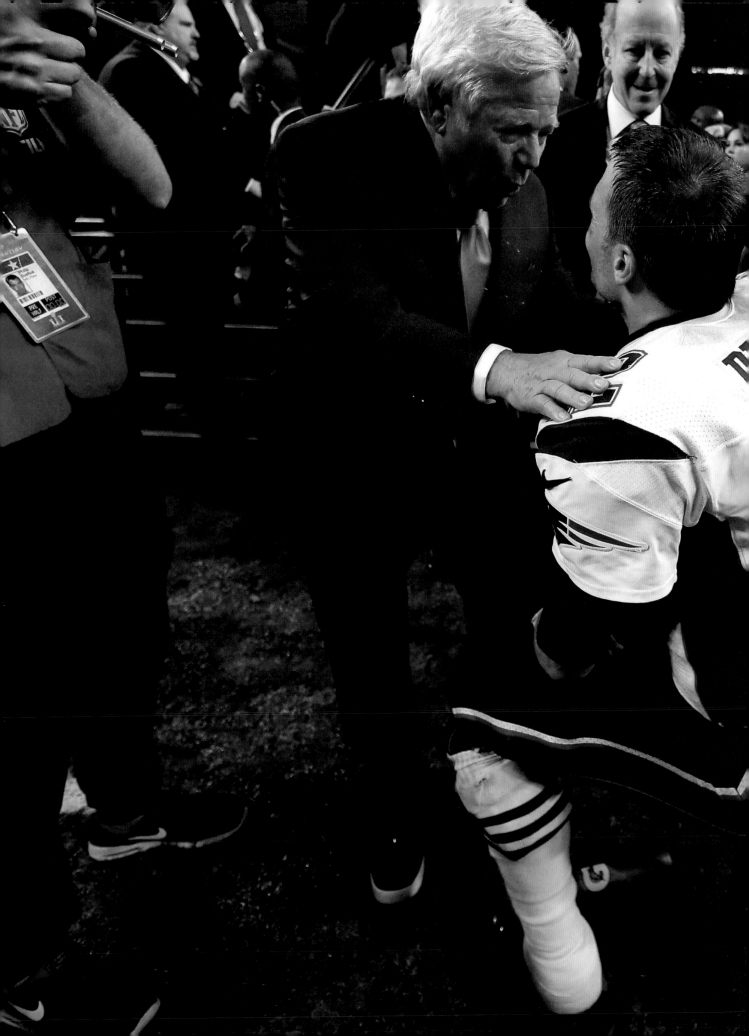

SIMPLY THE GREATEST NFL COACH EVER

Tony Dungy won a Super Bowl as a player for the 1978 Pittsburgh Steelers and as head coach of the 2006 Indianapolis Colts. He is an accomplished football man and a member of the Pro Football Hall of Fame's class of 2016. But when his Colts were facing Bill Belichick's Patriots during the height of their rivalry a decade ago, Dungy's last words of advice before his team took the field often sounded less like a coach motivating his players and more like the police sergeant on Hill Street Blues warning his cops: "Hey, let's be careful out there."

"I would tell them, 'We've got to survive the first quarter, because no matter what we prepare for we're going to see something we don't expect,' " recalls Dungy, who since retiring after the 2008 season has been an analyst on NBC's Sunday Night Football. "What I meant was if we don't dig ourselves too big of a hole in the first quarter, we'll be able to adjust."

Dungy's Colts actually had relative success against Belichick's Patriots, prevailing in four of nine matchups over Dungy's tenure. And the Colts' one playoff win in the teams' three postseason meetings stands in opposition to Dungy's credo: In the 2006 AFC Championship game, the host Colts fell behind by 18 points at 21-3, but rallied for a 38-34 victory. It remains one of the most disappointing outcomes of Belichick's extraordinary 17-year head coaching career with the Patriots.

Dungy, one of the most successful coaches of his time, was never sure what to expect from Belichick in part because they were not true peers. They were just contemporaries. Belichick's true peers are not the coaches of his time — they are the iconic coaches who don't just win multiple Super Bowls but get Super Bowl trophies named after them.

The question is not whether Belichick is the greatest coach of his time; that was all but determined a dozen years ago, when the Patriots won three Super Bowl titles in a four-year span. "[He] won three times in an era dramatically less congenial to creating a dynasty than before," argues NFL analyst Ron Jaworski in "The Education of a Coach," David Halberstam's 2005 biography of Belichick. The question now, after five Super Bowl titles, is whether he's the greatest coach of all time.

Belichick's fifth victory breaks a tie with Chuck Noll, the architect of the 1970s Steelers dynasty. Bill Walsh, the mastermind of the ingenious "West Coast offense" with the 1980s San Francisco 49ers, won three, as did the Washington Redskins' Joe Gibbs in the same era (and with three different quarterbacks, a remarkable feat). It should be noted that Vince Lombardi presided over the Green Bay Packers' victories in Super Bowl I and II — and his team also won three NFL championships before the advent of the Super Bowl.

Belichick has been to seven Super Bowls as the head coach of the Patriots. Only Don Shula (Colts, Dolphins) coached in as many as six, but he won just two. Belichick went to three more as an assistant to Bill Parcells (with the 1986 and '90 Giants and '96 Patriots, winning the first two); Parcells, inducted into the Pro Football Hall of Fame in 2013, never went to a Super Bowl without Belichick on his staff.

Ask Phil Simms, who faced Belichick's defenses in practice every day when he was the quarterback for those '80s Giants, and the question is already answered. "Is he going to go down as the greatest?" he says. "I don't know how you can even argue it."

What awes Belichick observers most is that he's doing all of this now, in an era of unparalleled competition. "The roster turnover is much higher than it has ever been before. The attrition rate is higher. [Players] get injured more frequently. The media focus is greater. There's wider access to game tape and a broader knowledge among coaches," says Bill Barnwell, an analytically minded football writer at ESPN.

Further, the worst teams get the higher draft picks, while a salary cap and free agency, which began in its current transaction-encouraging form in the mid '90s, make it significantly more difficult to keep a core intact than it was for the '60s Packers, '70s Steelers, or '80s Niners dynasties.

"It's not supposed to happen like this," says ESPN's Field Yates, who spent four summers as a scouting intern for the Patriots and also worked for the Kansas City Chiefs. "They're not supposed to be this good for that long. The league is designed to prevent this." Yet here's Belichick, the only coach to win at least 10 games for 14 straight seasons, compiling a 226-80 overall record in Foxborough.

It begins, many say, with his uncommon strategic malleability. Belichick deploys the Patriots' personnel in two fundamental ways: on offense, to expose and exploit an opponent's defensive flaws, and on defense, to take

understand how they do it," Dungy continues. "That's what's amazing to me, to be able to execute and be on your fundamentals and still change approaches week in and week out. I have no idea how they do it, but that to me is the genius."

Belichick, who entered the league as a $25-per-week special assistant with the 1975 Baltimore Colts, considers the perceived minutiae of the game more than relevant. He considers it essential, and his players had better, too. The best evidence that detailed preparation pays off came two years ago, when the Patriots won their fourth Super Bowl. With 26 seconds remaining, the Seattle Seahawks in possession

it up in practice and was required to do it again until he got it right. "That was their last walk-through play on the Saturday before the Super Bowl," former Patriots safety Rodney Harrison says. "These plays that we make, they just don't happen. You go over this stuff, and over it, and when it happens, you see it in slow motion on the field because you are ready."

Belichick's success, and his utter unwillingness to participate in any backslapping jocularity as he goes about it, has brought consternation from his contemporaries. His detractors cite two high-profile scandals — 2007's Spygate and 2015's Deflategate, which in sum

226-80

away what the opposing offense believes it does well. The defensive approach is one that was preached by Belichick's father, Steve, who in the 1950s authored a revered nuts-and-bolts how-to titled "Football Scouting Methods."

Their approach is contrary to what most teams do, which is to emphasize their own strengths, no matter what the opponent is doing to counter them. "The Patriots are exactly the opposite, and I don't

of the ball on the Patriots' 1-yard line, and the Patriots clinging to a 28-24 lead, obscure, undrafted rookie cornerback Malcolm Butler jumped a pass route at the goal line for an interception. It is arguably the most pivotal single play in Super Bowl history.

To some, it looked like blind luck. But in fact Belichick had hammered the play into Butler. It was revealed in a postseason documentary, "Do Your Job," that Butler had messed

cost the franchise more than $1 million and multiple draft picks — as evidence that his achievements have been aided by a loose and unsportsmanlike interpretation of certain rules. It also does not go unnoticed that his success has come with Brady, whose claim as the greatest quarterback of all time is as strong as Belichick's as a coach.

That conveniently ignores that Belichick is the one who »114

FROM 113 • drafted Brady in the sixth round of the 2000 NFL Draft, his first as Patriots head coach, even though his roster already had three quarterbacks and the team was $10.5 million over the salary cap. "People will always say he got lucky. I don't think it's luck," Simms says. "I think Bill Belichick saw something in Tom Brady." And it ignores the fact that Belichick cut other players to keep Brady on the active roster, turned to him when Drew Bledsoe was injured in 2001, and then retained him as the starter though Bledsoe was a popular figure who had signed a $103 million contract in the offseason.

Belichick has also succeeded in the times Brady has been absent. While Brady was suspended for the start of this season, the Patriots went 3-1 with their second- and third-string quarterbacks. And after Brady's knee injury in the 2008 opener put him out for the season, the Patriots went 11-5 with Matt Cassel, another Belichick find who hadn't even started in college.

Years after their careers are complete, players still marvel at Belichick's eye for detail and his ability to get the most out of his teams. "I left $4 million on the table to sign with Belichick, OK?" says Harrison, who came to the Patriots before the 2003 season after he was released by the San Diego Chargers. "When we sat down and I was a free agent, he said, 'I remember when we played you guys and you hit a guy and his helmet came off, one of the defensive backs, in warmups.' I said, 'Who the hell knows that?' "

"He remembered that," Harrison says. "What other coach remembers that? I left that money on the table because if he had that kind of memory about something so minute and forgettable, I couldn't imagine what he could teach me. I looked at my agent and said, 'Go work out a contract. This is where I want to be.' "

CHAD FINN • *Globe Staff*

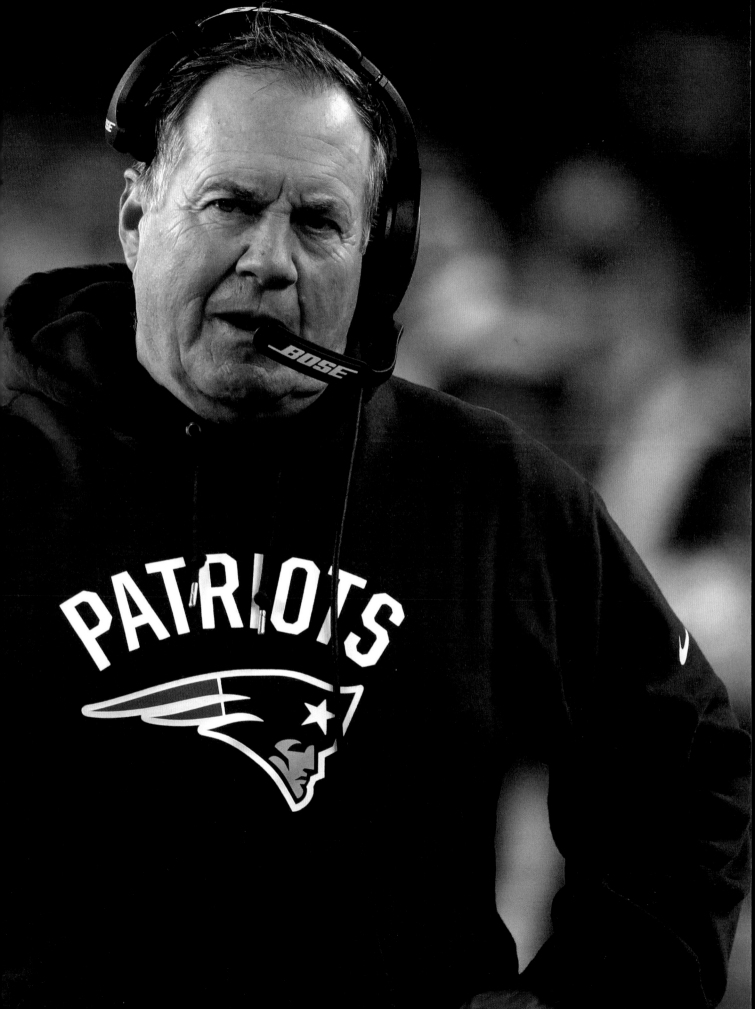

NOT AGELESS, BUT A WONDER

Tom Brady did not defy age this season, he knocked it down and left cleat marks.

The quarterback's age-39 season, which led to his record fifth Super Bowl victory, was statistically among the best of his 17-year career with the Patriots. His 2016 passer rating is tied for 10th best all-time in a season, at 112.2. He bettered that rating only once in his career, in 2007, when the Patriots became the only NFL team to win all 16 regular-season games.

What's maybe most remarkable about his 2016 performance is that it came at an age by which many other luminaries of the position — Dan Marino, Joe Montana, and John Elway, to name three — already had retired.

Beyond maniacal workouts to maintain his VO2 max (the amount of oxygen an athlete can use under all-out exertion), the right DNA, and a dose of good luck, there is likely a combination of factors that have contributed to Brady's successful late career.

"It doesn't mean that he's not aging," said Wojtek Chodzko-Zajko, a kinesiology professor at the University of Illinois at Urbana-Champaign. "It means he's utilizing some of the strengths that happen with increased experience and increased wisdom to compensate for some of the physical changes that occur."

It is a theory endorsed by Warren Moon, another Methuselah of the NFL.

Moon was selected to the 1997 Pro Bowl at age 41, after a season in which he threw 25 touchdown passes for the Seattle Seahawks. By age 39, he said, his athleticism had clearly declined. "I wasn't the same runner or scrambler," Moon, now 60, said in a phone interview. "But having seen everything defensively that you can see, it makes the game a lot slower, which makes you a little bit faster. Not physically faster. Your mind reacts faster."

That seemed the case this season for Brady, who threw 28 touchdown passes and just two interceptions in 12 games. NFL rules changes designed to reduce dangerous blows to the quarterback's head and knees may also be contributing to Brady's longevity.

Brady has mostly avoided serious injuries, beyond a 2008 ACL tear that cost him 15 games and inspired an NFL rule change to forbid defenders knocked to the ground from lunging into the quarterback's lower legs.

Brady works fanatically on exercises to maintain flexibility, a trait he said keeps him healthy. Brady is also known for his obsessive "anti-inflammation" diet, which avoids white sugar and flour, dairy and caffeine, as well as things widely considered healthy, such as most fruit, tomatoes, peppers, and mushrooms, his personal chef told Boston.com last year.

Injuries can compound as a quarterback ages, said Moon, who was in the NFL until age 44. Moon considers himself "very lucky that I only had a couple of different fractures. I never had anything major, like a major knee injury or major shoulder separation in my passing arm. You look at Peyton Manning and the neck surgeries he had over his career. It was amazing he was able to come back and play the way he did. But at some point that's going to catch up with you. And you saw when he kind of hit the wall, it went fast."

Manning retired at 39 after a 2015 season in which his team won the Super Bowl but he finished with a career-low passer rating.

Brady has suggested he wants to play until he's nearly 50. That's probably too old, Moon said, but he thinks Brady and Drew Brees, the 38-year-old New Orleans Saints quarterback, "could definitely play until they're around 45."

"There's no reason they shouldn't be able to play at a high level longer — you can if you take care of yourself," Moon said. "That's one of the reasons I think Tom has been so successful. His training regimen is second to none ... and he's one of the most competitive people you ever want to meet. You combine all those things and there's a reason this guy is still playing at the top of his game."

MARK ARSENAULT • *Globe Staff*
(with Andrew Joseph of STAT contributing)

THIS DEFENSE NEVER RESTED

As the regular season wound down to its final weekend, Patriots linebacker Dont'a Hightower was asked if the team's defensive players were aware that New England led the NFL in fewest points allowed.

"Hell, yeah," replied Hightower, who with his mates went on to break the Seattle Seahawks' reign of four seasons (2012-15) leading the league in points against. The Patriots allowed 250 points in 16 games, a 15.6-point average, more than two points better than the New York Giants (17.8) and nearly three points better than Seattle (18.3), which finished third.

"That hasn't really been our goal, it's just something that's happened on account of our play," said Hightower. "But our job is to keep the offense from scoring the ball — so any time we can do that and do it well we're winning."

The Patriots' 15.6 points-allowed average was the best in a season by anyone since the Seahawks allowed 14.4 in 2013. It also helped New England post a league-best 12.0-point-per-game differential, when combined with their 27.6-point scoring average.

When Hightower joined the Patriots as a first-round draft pick in 2012, Matt Patricia was just taking over as the team's defensive coordinator. Hightower credits Patricia with much of his development into a Pro Bowl selection at linebacker.

"Matty P. has definitely helped," Hightower said. "He was one of the guys who helped me move along at an accelerated pace, as far as getting me to understand the defense and what he really wanted me to do. I love him. He's a great coach and even a better man."

Patricia, 42, is a graduate of Rensselaer Polytechnic Institute (RPI), in Troy, N.Y., where he was an offensive lineman who majored in aeronautical engineering. He coached at his alma mater, then at Amherst College and Syracuse University before joining the Patriots in 2004.

Asked about Patricia's in-game coaching adjustments, Hightower said, "It really is amazing, and a lot of times early in the game, there are plays that give you trouble and you know you're not able to get it done. We're getting those adjustments on the sideline, and those can really make or break you.

"He's a smart guy. He's a rocket scientist, man. For him to be able to diagnose those things is truly amazing."

Hightower also credits the Patriots' success to attention to detail, including tackling technique.

"We take a lot of pride in it," Hightower said. "It seems like a simple task, just getting somebody down on the ground, but it's a lot harder than it looks.

"That was a problem early in the year that we wanted to get fixed. A big part of us playing the way we've been playing is because we've been tackling well."

The criticism of the unit peaked after the Seahawks scored 31 points on the Patriots in Week 10. Since then, the defense has been stingier than ever — including its effort against Pittsburgh in the AFC title game, when the Patriots held the explosive Steelers to 17 points.

The Patriots also have had to adjust to the losses through trades of linebackers Chandler Jones and Jamie Collins, while bringing in newcomers such as Trey Flowers, Chris Long, Shea McClellin, and Kyle Van Noy.

"I feel like the communication aspect of that is big, and it's a lot better," Hightower said. "I think guys have gotten comfortable.

"Whenever you get that, you can play a lot faster and kind of anticipate things. You try and get a jump on the offense. I think we're finally at that point."

The defense also didn't allow a touchdown for a stretch of more than 140 minutes over Weeks 14-17 — nearly 10 quarters of play.

Points per game was the only defensive category the Patriots led the NFL in, although, according to coach Bill Belichick, no other statistic matters as much in winning.

"No. 1 is points, No. 2 is turnovers," the Patriots coach said after a 41-3 victory over the Jets in late December.

JIM MCBRIDE • *Globe Staff*

GROUND CONTROL FOR MAJOR TOM

Bill Belichick's postgame locker-room speech was interesting to watch following the Patriots' 27-0 dismantling of the Texans in Week 3, and not just because it offered a rare glimpse of an unfiltered Belichick.

Look in the background of the video posted on the Patriots' website and you'll notice quarterback Jacoby Brissett and offensive coordinator Josh McDaniels engaged in a full-on bro hug, standing with their arms around each others' waists after Brissett led the Patriots to a big win.

"It was just an exciting time," Brissett said. "You don't really think about that stuff. It just happens in the spur of the moment."

Except you never would have seen the old McDaniels, the wunderkind offensive coordinator who became a head coach at age 33, being embraced by his players. McDaniels freely admits that the younger version of himself was too focused on doing things his way and figuring out the perfect play for third and 6, and didn't put enough value in interpersonal relationships.

He tried to be Belichick Jr. in Denver when he was hired as head coach in 2009, but the Broncos quickly grew weary of the Napoleon act, and fired McDaniels before the end of his second season with an 11-17 record. Former Broncos Pro Bowl defensive end Alfred Williams called him "Hurricane Josh," and

Denver fans thought McDaniels was just a Patriots operative seeking to destroy the Broncos from the inside.

Six years later, McDaniels appears to have successfully rehabilitated his image, and then some. Now 40, McDaniels is expected by many to be an NFL head coach again soon. McDaniels turned down an opportunity to be the 49ers coach in January, saying, "At this time, it's best for my family and myself to remain here," in New England, making Patriots fans and a certain quarterback very happy.

Tom Brady isn't surprised by the interest McDaniels has garnered.

"I think he's the best in the NFL," said Brady in early January. "For me, I could never be the player that I am without him and without him challenging me every week. I have so much confidence in him as a coach and his abilities, the way that he leads our offense, he's spectacular. It would be tough to lose him."

McDaniels's résumé boasts offenses that have finished among the top five in scoring in each of his last four seasons, and he has helped Brady turn in some of the best seasons of his career in his late 30s.

But perhaps most impressive was McDaniels's work this season with the Patriots' young backup quarterbacks, Jimmy Garoppolo and Brissett. That the Patriots went 3-1 without Brady or, for all intents and purposes, Rob Gronkowski,

speaks highly of McDaniels's ability to overcome adversity, develop young quarterbacks, and craft game plans that are tailored to a player's strengths.

His friends say that McDaniels knows he'll only get one more chance to be an NFL head coach, that the opportunity has to be just right, and that he hasn't been dying to leave New England.

"I love where I'm at," he said on WEEI at midseason. "I think we all have aspirations to grow and get better and improve and eventually move up and what have you. Who knows? Maybe that day happens, maybe it doesn't. But I know this ... I feel like I have one of the best jobs in the world."

McDaniels has owned up to a lot of his mistakes in Denver. Married and with four children ranging from 3 to 12 years old, he said he spends more time at his son's flag football games and takes better care of himself. McDaniels has become close friends with the Patriots' team chaplain, saying "he's got me to embrace how important faith is in my life," and doesn't come down too hard on his players and assistants when things don't work out.

Put it this way, if NFL teams never hired coaches who failed with a previous team, then Belichick never would have been hired by the Patriots in 2000.

BEN VOLIN • *Globe Staff*

NEW ENGLAND

WR | Danny
AMENDOLA
Texas Tech
5'11 | 190 lbs
exp. 8 yrs.

C | David
ANDREWS
Georgia
6'3 | 295 lbs
exp. 2 yrs.

TE | Martellus
BENNETT
Texas A&M
6'6 | 275 lbs
exp. 8 yrs.

RB | LeGarrette
BLOUNT
Oregon
6'0 | 250 lbs
exp. 7 yrs.

RB | Brandon
BOLDEN
Mississippi
5'11 | 220 lbs
exp. 5 yrs.

QB | Tom
BRADY
Michigan
6'4 | 225 lbs
exp. 17 yrs.

QB | Jacoby
BRISSETT
North Carolina State
6'4 | 235 lbs
exp. R

OL | Marcus
CANNON
Texas Christian
6'5 | 335 lbs
exp. 6 yrs.

FB | James
DEVELIN
Brown
6'3 | 255 lbs
exp. 4 yrs

WR | Julian
EDELMAN
Kent State
5'10 | 200 lbs
exp. 8 yrs

OL | Cameron
FLEMING
Stanford
6'6 | 320 lbs
exp. 3 yrs.

WR | Michael
FLOYD
Notre Dame
6'2 | 220 lbs
exp. 5 yrs

RB | D.J.
FOSTER
Arizona State
6'0 | 195 lbs
exp. R

QB | Jimmy
GAROPPOLO
Eastern Illinois
6'2 | 225 lbs
exp. 3 yrs

K | Stephen
GOSTKOWSKI
Memphis
6'1 | 215 lbs
exp. 11 yrs

TE | Rob
GRONKOWSKI*
Arizona
6'6 | 265 lbs
exp. 7 yrs

WR | Chris
HOGAN
Monmouth (N.J.)
6'1 | 210 lbs
exp. 4 yrs

G | Tré
JACKSON*
Florida State
6'4 | 320 lbs
exp. 2 yrs

OL | Ted
KARRAS
Illinois
6'4 | 305 lbs
exp. R

TE | Matt
LENGEL
Eastern Kentucky
6'7 | 266 lbs
exp. 1 yr.

RB | Dion
LEWIS
Pittsburgh
5'8 | 195 lbs
exp. 5 yrs

OL | Shaq
MASON
Georgia Tech
6'1 | 310 lbs
exp. 2 yrs.

WR | Malcolm
MITCHELL
Georgia
5'11 | 200 lbs
exp. R

TE | Greg
SCRUGGS*
Louisville
6'3 | 277 lbs
exp. 4 yrs

WR | Matthew
SLATER
UCLA
6'0 | 205 lbs
exp. 9 yrs

T | Nate
SOLDER
Colorado
6'8 | 325 lbs
exp. 6 yrs.

G | Joe
THUNEY
North Carolina State
6'4 | 295 lbs
exp. R

T | Sebastian
VOLLMER*
Houston
6'8 | 320 lbs
exp. 8 yrs

OL | LaAdrian
WADDLE
Texas Tech
6'6 | 315 lbs
exp. 4 yrs

RB | James
WHITE
Wisconsin
5'10 | 205 lbs
exp. 3 yrs

* INJURED

PATRIOTS 2016

P | Ryan
ALLEN
Louisiana Tech
6'2 | 220 lbs
exp. 4 yrs

DL | Alan
BRANCH
Michigan
6'6 | 350 lbs
exp. 10 yrs

DL | Malcom
BROWN
Texas
6'2 | 320 lbs
exp. 2 yrs

CB | Malcolm
BUTLER
West Alabama
5'11 | 190 lbs
exp. 3 yrs

LS | Joe
CARDONA
Navy
6'3 | 245 lbs
exp. 2 yrs

S | Patrick
CHUNG
Oregon
5'11 | 215 lbs
exp. 8 yrs

DB | Justin
COLEMAN
Tennessee
5'11 | 190 lbs
exp. 2 yrs

DB | Nate
EBNER
Ohio State
6'0 | 220 lbs
exp. 5 yrs

DL | Trey
FLOWERS
Arkansas
6'2 | 265 lbs
exp. 2 yrs

LB | Jonathan
FREENY*
Rutgers
6'2 | 255 lbs
exp. 5 yrs

DL | Geneo
GRISSOM
Oklahoma
6'4 | 265 lbs
exp. 2 yrs

DB | Duron
HARMON
Rutgers
6'1 | 205 lbs
exp. 4 yrs

LB | Dont'a
HIGHTOWER
Alabama
6'3 | 265 lbs
exp. 5 yrs

CB | Cyrus
JONES
Alabama
5'10 | 200 lbs
exp. R

DB | Jonathan
JONES
Auburn
5'10 | 190 lbs
exp. R

DB | Brandon
KING
Auburn
6'2 | 220 lbs
exp. 2 yrs

DE | Chris
LONG
Virginia
6'3 | 270 lbs
exp. 9 yrs

LB | Shea
McCLELLIN
Boise State
6'3 | 250 lbs
exp. 5 yrs

DB | Devin
McCOURTY
Rutgers
5'10 | 195 lbs
exp. 7 yrs

LB | Barkevious
MINGO
LSU
6'4 | 240 lbs
exp. 4 yrs

LB | Rob
NINKOVICH
Purdue
6'2 | 260 lbs
exp. 11 yrs

DB | Jordan
RICHARDS
Stanford
5'11 | 210 lbs
exp. 2 yrs

LB | Elandon
ROBERTS
Houston
5'11 | 235 lbs
exp. R

DB | Eric
ROWE
Utah
6'1 | 205 lbs
exp. 2 yrs

CB | Logan
RYAN
Rutgers
5'11 | 195 lbs
exp. 4 yrs

DL | Jabaal
SHEARD
Pittsburgh
6'3 | 265 lbs
exp. 6 yrs

DT | Vincent
VALENTINE
Nebraska
6'2 | 320 lbs
exp. R

LB | Kyle
VAN NOY
Brigham Young
6'3 | 243 lbs
exp. 3 yrs

HEAD COACH
Bill
BELICHICK
Wesleyan
W-L: 238-115
exp: 22 years

Tom Brady warms up before Super Bowl LI at NRG Stadium in Houston. Brady went on to break Super Bowl passing records with 43 completions in 62 attempts for 466 yards.

Patriots fans put on their game faces during Super Bowl weekend in Houston, which included a fan experience at a nearby convention center.

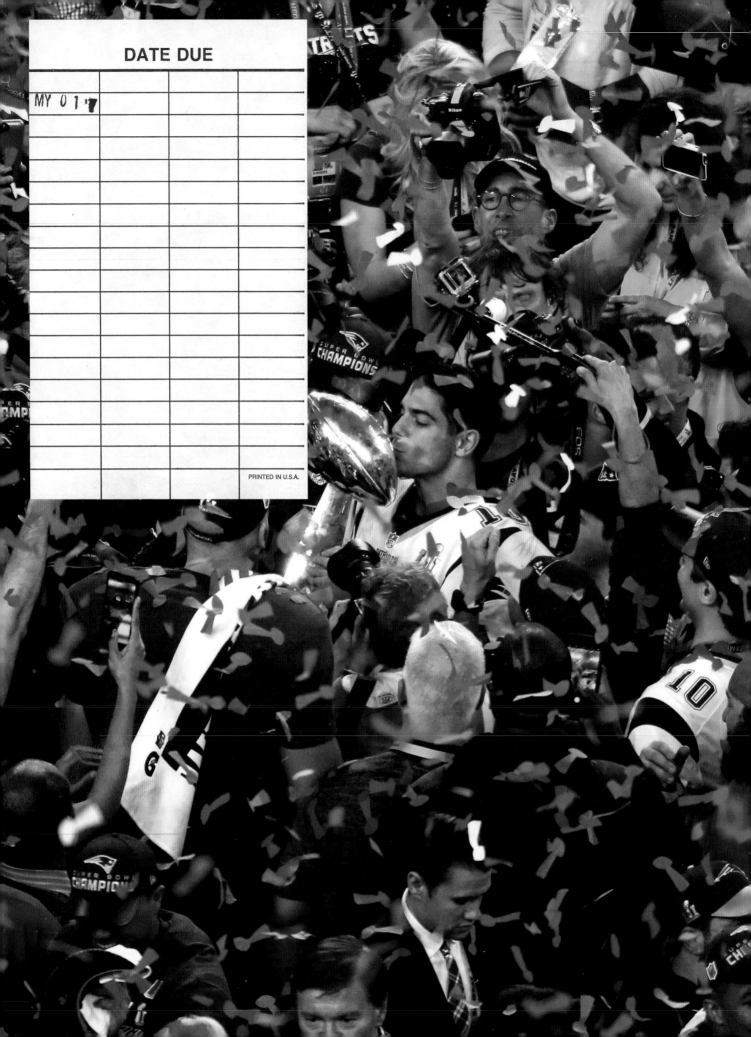

DATE DUE

MY 01 '7			

PRINTED IN U.S.A.